Marina Caldarone

is a freelance theatre and radio drama director who has also been actively involved in actor training since 1985. She is Drama Director for Crying Out Loud, a production company making CDs for actors entering the voice industry, as well as working as an acting coach, and lecturing regularly on theatre.

Maggie Lloyd-Williams

has acted in a number of plays at the National Theatre as well as at the Soho Theatre, the Tricycle and Shakespeare's Globe. She has also appeared in several television series such as *Secret Diary of a Call Girl*, *Murphy's Law*, *The Vice*, *Red Cap*, *Silent Witness* and *Casualty*.

A
C
T
I
O
N
S

Actions: The Actors' Thesaurus is now available as an app for the iPhone, iPad and iPod touch.

The app includes the entire thesaurus, with various different ways of searching for the right action and navigating through the word lists, the ability to bookmark your favourite actions, and a comprehensive introduction about the technique of actioning.

ACTIONS

The Actors'
Thesaurus

MARINA CALDARONE
and
MAGGIE LLOYD-WILLIAMS

NICK HERN BOOKS
London
www.nickhernbooks.co.uk

A Nick Hern Book

Actions – The Actors' Thesaurus
first published in Great Britain in 2004
as a paperback original by Nick Hern Books
Limited, The Glasshouse, 49a Goldhawk Road,
London W12 8QP

Reprinted in this revised edition 2011, 2012, 2013, 2014

Copyright © 2004, 2011 Marina Caldarone
and Maggie Lloyd-Williams

Foreword copyright © 2004 Terry Johnson

Marina Caldarone and Maggie Lloyd-Williams
have asserted their moral right to be identified
as the authors of this work

Cover Design by Ned Hoste, 2H

Typeset by Country Setting,
Kingsdown, Kent CT14 8ES

Printed and bound in Great Britain
by CPI Antony Rowe, Chippenham, Wiltshire

British Library Cataloguing Data for this book
is available from the British Library

ISBN 978 1 85459 674 1

To
Lucy McNulty
and
Elaine Roundacre

I once met Sinead Cusack at a Christmas party. The previous year she'd been offered a job by Max Stafford-Clark. She'd heard about the way he works. (Max requires his actors to action each line of text and to annotate their scripts, sitting around a table for two to three weeks of rehearsal to achieve this.)

Sinead had told him, 'I'd love to work with you, but I know how you work and I have to say up-front I can't do it and I won't do it.'

Max replied, 'Try it for a week.'

'No.'

'I really want you to play this part. Give me four days.'

'No.'

'Three days.'

'Absolutely not.'

'Give me two days and if you're not happy, we'll do it your way.'

A big gesture from the immaculate Max. So finally, consigning the first two days of rehearsal to what she imagined would be a complete waste of her time, Sinead agreed to do the job.

She told me, 'I did it his way for two days, then three days, then a week. Two weeks later we were still at it.' She took a sip of mulled wine, tasting the memory, then in her gorgeous liquid brogue said, 'How did I ever act before that?'

I have worked with actors whose foreheads hit the table at the very mention of an action. I have worked with actors who energetically resist the idea that rational thought might be part of their creative process. But I have helped transform some young actors by converting them to a belief in Actioning. More instructively, I have worked with many actors (and I include in this all the best ones) for whom actions are a second language. Not a foreign language or an exotic one, but a technical articulation of the elusively human. A good actor talks about actions like a builder-decorator talks about the nature of nails or the colour of paint. Actions can lead an actor from confusion to clarity, from muddle to magnificence, from the clichéd to the complex.

This thesaurus of riches can help the actor develop that language. The final section is a genuine tool, using which the actor can analyse any one moment of his character's journey, define instinctively the basic polarities of feeling towards another character, then select the intensity of that feeling, and thus arrive at a choice selection of appropriate transitive verbs.

It sounds complex, but so is dancing the salsa, and that only takes an hour or so to get into the musculature. If you want to act, or act better, actions will take you a long way on the journey to excellence.

TERRY JOHNSON

Actions – The Actors' Thesaurus aims to clarify a widely used rehearsal and performance technique, known by different names, but here called Actioning.

Actioning provides the **stimulation** for the actor to directly play each line of the text and develop alternative ways of bringing their character to life. The technique encourages performances with accurate and dramatic communication between characters.

Actioning heightens the actor's **spontaneity**, discouraging him or her from monotonously and automatically replicating a tone. Everyone has seen productions – particularly of Shakespeare's plays – where, if they were completely honest, both audience and players alike don't have a clue about what's going on; it's all 'sound and fury signifying nothing.' Actioning should keep the actors 'in the moment' and deter what Peter Brook calls 'deadly' acting, where nothing is going on, just words being spoken.

If the actor plays a real and specific action on each sentence then, even though the audience are unlikely to be able to identify the technique or the individual action, the work will be interesting and absolutely watchable because of its precision. Actioning enforces a **specificity** which can liberate the actor's performance and ensure a cohesive integrated character with each moment leading naturally onto the next.

Actioning is a starting point for use in the rehearsal room and for private textual analysis. It really comes to fruition in performance, affording actors the **self-confidence** to develop and refine their choices continuously. Actioning keeps the text alive by ensuring the drama is active and subject to constant redefinition.

If a whole company takes an hour to explore the principle at the start of rehearsals, a shared dramaturgical language is established. This **synchronisation** can save rehearsal time and facilitate more efficient communication.

Stimulation – Spontaneity – Specificity
Self-confidence – Synchronisation

Actioning is primarily for actors – for established professionals and beginners alike, for students or amateur actors, for those with training and those without. Actioning can also be useful for music theatre performers, for actors wrestling with audition speeches, for those who have to breathe life into a one-dimensional television or radio commercial, or for those who have been performing a play for months and need to re-invigorate their performance.

This book can also be used by academic students of drama to deconstruct a script for its sub-textual dynamic.

The Origins of Actioning

Actioning comes from Stanislavski (1863-1938), the Russian actor/director/theorist who formulated a revolutionary acting methodology which seeks to enhance psychological depth and emotional truth in performance. His system, still studied and practised widely around the world, acted as a catalyst for other approaches to acting, including the American Method.

In his work (primarily at the Moscow Art Theatre), Stanislavski pioneered a series of exercises and rules which would allow actors to access their emotions more freely and maintain the essential but elusive creative state.

Concentrating on Actioning may be many actors' way of short-circuiting all elements of the rather more complex and more psychologically demanding system. Nonetheless, knowledge of key elements of Stanislavski's system is vital before being able to begin your work on Actioning.

Units and Objectives

Finding an action for a particular moment or line of text is dependent upon understanding the Stanislavskian concept of units and objectives (sometimes called episodes and tasks). In each unit of the text, you must decide on your objective (what your character wants) before defining the action (how your character sets out to get it).

Begin by breaking the scene up into units, each containing a single defined objective. Stanislavski makes a useful analogy in *An Actor Prepares*. For him, the process of dividing a play into its component units is like breaking up a cooked chicken so that it can be eaten. If eaten portion by portion, then the whole chicken can ultimately be devoured. Similarly, the scene is broken into its separate 'portions' or units in order to be investigated. Each unit has its own title, which describes what that unit is about, and each character has his or her own objective at the heart of that unit. Like units, which can be major (whole sections of text) or minor (a single word or short sentence), so the characters' objectives are major or minor according to how the second-to-second minutiae of the scene develops.

Stanislavski warns: 'You should not try to express the meaning of your objectives in terms of a noun. That can be used for a unit but the objective must always be a verb.' Take the word 'power', for example. Turn it into an objective:

'I want power.' On its own, this is too general and, therefore, unplayable. Introduce something more definitely active and the objective is better defined: 'I want to do *something* to obtain power.' The '*something*' element of the equation helps you find your action for the unit. The actions are what you do to obtain what you want; they are the tactics you employ.

Actioning Today

The widespread use of Actioning in the professional theatre seems to have developed in Europe and the US over the last fifty years, a theory handed down by word of mouth through generations of actors and directors. The principles of Actioning are now taught at many drama schools and conservatoires and, whilst it cannot be assumed that all actors share the same dramatic language and practise the same rehearsal techniques, it is safe to say that increasing numbers of performers are aware of and use the process.

Certainly with many directors using Actioning as a fundamental rehearsal technique (the eminent British director, Max Stafford-Clark, famously spends the first few weeks of rehearsals Actioning the text), it is a process that every actor should recognise and feel comfortable with.

Although the theory of Actioning has been laid down before, this is the first time a thesaurus of transitive verbs has been specifically compiled to facilitate the actor's work and to support this theory.

How to Action the Text

What we say and what we think or mean don't always correspond. Take the most straightforward non sequitur: 'Would you like a coffee?' You could say that the speaker's objective is simply 'I want to offer you a drink' but, more likely, there are a whole host of deeper impulses between the two individuals operating underneath the surface. The objective is more likely to be along the lines of 'I want you to be relaxed', 'I want to show you I'm a caring person', 'I want you to stay the night' and so on.

Actioning offers an immediate way of *achieving* this objective. The action word is a succinct and specific transitive verb which describes what your character is actually *doing* to another character. As the old saying goes, actions really can speak louder than words.

'Would you like a coffee?' could be played in many ways, according to the context of the scene and the character's objective. Different action words might be *seduce, welcome, dominate, befriend, admire, fear, disgrace, manipulate*... The choice is virtually limitless – but must always be determined by the character's objective.

Identifying Action Words

Transitive Verbs

An action word must always be a transitive verb.

A transitive or active verb is a verb ('a doing word') that you can actively do to someone else. It is always in the present tense and transitional, expressing an action that carries over from you (the subject) to the person you're speaking to (the object).

A useful way to identify if a verb is transitive or not is to place it between the words 'I' and 'you' and see if the sentence makes sense.

So, in the case of *charm*, *encourage* and *cherish*, 'I *charm* you', 'I *encourage* you', 'I *cherish* you' all make sense and so those three verbs must be transitive. They each express an action between characters and can define the impulse under each sentence.

Transitive Verb 'Wannabes'

Some verbs feel and sound as though they ought to be active, but in fact are not and cannot be used as actions. They will not adhere to the 'I do something to you' principle.

For example, 'I *interfere* with you' is not active since 'with' disrupts the principle. This may seem purist, but it will force you to be more specific, as there are many ways one can 'interfere with' someone. So, you might choose to play I *disorientate* you, *disrupt* you, *muddle* you, *upset* you, *interrupt* you, *impede* you, *hamper* you; all of which are transitive.

When the verb requires a noun, it is not transitive. For example, *abate* needs a noun – 'I *abate* your fears' – for the sentence to work. Similarly, *allocate*, *concede* and *assign* ('I *allocate* you a place', 'I *concede* the argument to you' or 'I *assign* you the task') cannot be action words.

Choosing the Action

Look at the text offered to you. Start by clarifying what your character wants: their objective. Then choose a transitive verb for each sentence which helps the character achieve that objective.

So if A says 'Would you like a coffee?' and the objective is to make B so comfortable he stays a bit longer, then A might choose to play 'I *befriend* you' or she could be more seductive and play 'I *beguile* you' as her tactic for achieving the objective.

Every action has a different flavour in the mouth, however similar the word looks on the page or synonymous you might think it is. It is your job to locate exactly the right word for the moment and then to play it.

An action is not necessarily right or wrong – instead, it is helpful or unhelpful in fulfilling the objective, enlivening the performance and telling the story. An action may or perhaps *should* change throughout rehearsal and performance. At the early stage of rehearsals, it is better to be instinctive in your choice and then finalise and hone the action later.

Playing the Action

Try the action out. Put the words of the text into your mouth. Drop your action in, speak your line now invested with your action. Speak the action out loud before continuing with the sentence. This can be done in the first person ("I tease you: 'Are you the lady of the house?'") or the third person ("Viola teases Olivia: 'Are you the lady of the house?'").

How does it feel? Try some other verbs, play around a little. Find the verb that feels perfect, the one that makes sense in your heart as well as in your head for that moment in the scene and to achieve that objective.

Another way to play around with getting used to the system is to speak your line to a couple of friends or colleagues, neutrally, with nothing invested in it. Then drop your action in, keeping it to yourself. Speak the sentence again, now invested with the action. Can your friends locate what action you are playing? How close are they? Try again. Can you do anything to make your playing more precise and the action clearer? The results of this exercise should not be considered a judgement on whether you can act! Rather, it is a fun way of experimenting with how many ways you can play an action, and how effective those versions are.

Actioning is designed to help your imagination, not replace it. Stay instinctive, stay open, surprise yourself by playing something that you wouldn't normally play, have fun. When something doesn't work, try another option until the alchemy is right. The ways in which you achieve your objective could be as many as the imagination is infinite.

You could work in reverse and decide to identify your objective only *after* having actioned each sentence thoroughly and found the most appropriate action word. It's up to you.

The Actioning Mantra

One thought. One sentence. One breath. One action…

– We choose an action for each whole thought.

– A whole thought is comprised within a whole sentence.

– This sentence should be spoken with one breath.

– And each breath should contain one action.

…One thought. One sentence. One breath. One action.

Actions in the Rehearsal Room

Some companies sit around a table for a large proportion of rehearsals deciding together what each action for each sentence should be, before putting any of the play onto its feet. They are mapping out the play's journey, exploring all the characters' journeys en route to the desired destination. They are building up a common interpretation and language, so that during the production run, changes can be made by the cast to enliven and invigorate what could become staid.

Other companies might touch on the language of Actioning early on, but not explore the play exhaustively by this method, only asking what actions are at play when things become stale.

The individual actor might choose to locate their character's actions for themselves when investigating the script: an emotional limbering-up before meeting the other characters in the rehearsal room. They might not mention to anyone else what their process is; after all, there are as many rehearsal processes as actors in the company.

Whilst Actioning can be applied by the solo actor in their preparation for playing a role, it works best when employed by a whole company. The text is re-active and works with (or against) text spoken by other characters. When a company works together to define their actions, there is the opportunity to play with and explore different actions, pick up ideas from one another and bounce off the actions of other characters. Intentions, meanings, possible actions and avenues for your character that might otherwise have been missed are revealed when Actioning together.

Whilst in life we do not generally know or understand people's true actions, objectives and intentions towards us, Actioning affords us this unique privilege and paves the way to a more inspired and dynamic performance by all actors in the company.

Actioning a Soliloquy

But what happens if the actor is not speaking to anyone? What if the actor is working on an audition speech or soliloquy and needs to enliven and motivate it?

Let's look at the first part of probably the most famous soliloquy of all time.

Hamlet
by Shakespeare (Act 3 Scene 1)

To be, or not to be – that is the question;
Whether 'tis nobler in the mind to suffer
The slings and arrows of outrageous fortune,
Or to take arms against a sea of troubles,
And by opposing end them. To die, to sleep,
No more; and by a sleep to say we end
The heartache and the thousand natural shocks
That flesh is heir to. 'Tis a consummation
Devoutly to be wished. To die, to sleep;
To sleep, perchance to dream. Ay, there's the rub.
For in that sleep of death what dreams may come
When we have shuffled off this mortal coil
Must give us pause.

Externalising the Actions

Try imagining the space inhabited with people
from the character's life and direct each complete
thought to those people. This is not literal, it
is imaginative. One *imagines* directing each
sentence to X so that there is a concrete and
specific impetus and objective on each line.

1) To be, or not to be – that is the question;
2) Whether 'tis nobler in the mind to suffer
The slings and arrows of outrageous fortune,
Or to take arms against a sea of troubles,
And by opposing end them. 3) To die, to sleep,
No more; and by a sleep to say we end
The heartache and the thousand natural
shocks
That flesh is heir to.

For example:

1) Addressed to his father (alive or dead) and
   he might play the action: to *defy*.

2) Addressed to Claudius and he might play
   the action: to *challenge*.

3) Addressed to Ophelia and he might play the
   action: to *comfort*.

Internalising the Actions

Divide the character into his or her own lower and higher self, each having a very different identity. Then, address the text and the objective to these different aspects of oneself, as if talking to a separate person.

> 4) 'Tis a consummation
> Devoutly to be wished. To die, to sleep;
> 5) To sleep, perchance to dream. 6) Ay, there's the rub.
> 7) For in that sleep of death what dreams may come
> When we have shuffled off this mortal coil
> Must give us pause.

For example:

4) Directed at his lowest self – the scared, childlike boy inside Hamlet – and he might use the action: to *awaken*.

5) Directed at his higher self and he might play: to *comfort* or to *console*.

6) Directed to his own collapsed self-esteem and he might play: to *entertain*.

7) Directed to the moralising philosopher within, so he might play: to *elevate*.

Even if the audience doesn't fully understand every word or thought of a complex speech, the tonal variety and textural depth provided by these actions conveys acting which is truthful and specific, rather than phoney and generalised.

Introduction to the Revised Edition

We have been delighted by the success of *Actions*, and inundated with feedback. As a result, for this revised edition, we have removed some of the arguably 'unactable' actions, and added some new ones. Some of the added actions are quite colloquial (eg. to *pigeonhole* or to *rumble* – as in 'to find someone out'), but are hopefully usable nonetheless. Choosing actions is a subjective process, but the following tools might help you to bring some more specificity to your choices.

The Qualification

You can make your action more specific by 'qualifying' it with a descriptive term. It defines 'the *how* of the *what*' by inserting an adverb into the action. It's impossible to provide a list of these qualifications as the list is as extensive as your imagination.

As an example, take the line 'I wish you would stay', and the chosen action: to *implore*. If your character is ruled by conformity and the desire to be polite, then you might qualify the action so it becomes: to *implore with appropriate decorum*; if you are sarcastic or belittling it might be: to *implore with disdain*. Other options might be to *implore... with unbridled lust... with regret... with commanding superiority... with joy... with fundamental commitment... with honesty... with blind rage... with self-righteousness...* The options are endless.

Finding a qualification is about bringing added complexity to the action, which enables you to explore two tactics and allow two energies to resonate in that one moment. It can make your acting choices easier to access, more specific to play, and more fun.

The Action Spectrum

Something else to think about is the Action Spectrum: is it possible to play an action on an emotional spectrum of 1–100% (or 1 to 10 if you prefer)? There's no need to be too specific; it would be an almost entirely academic exercise to distinguish between playing at 68% as opposed to 72%, for instance. But as a measure of stepping up the volume or intensity (or vice versa), it can be a useful tool. Continuing the earlier example, it would obviously be different if you were playing 'I wish you would stay' with the action – to *implore* – at the level of 90% intensity, as opposed to a level of 40%.

These additional techniques don't detract from the essential simplicity of the Actioning process, and should only be used if they're helpful to you and enhance your work. Anything that extends the investigative process is all good!

M.C. and M.L.W., 2011

How to Use *The Actors' Thesaurus*

This thesaurus is designed to extend the actor's vocabulary when Actioning the text. It is not totally comprehensive, nor will it choose actions for you, but it should be used to open up your imagination and help you to refine your choices. It is intended that the actor navigates his or her way through the word list by making simple choices which logically lead to a final, specific, accurately defined transitive verb.

Each individual actor (and director) will have differing personal approaches to how they use Actioning as a rehearsal and performance technique. Some will want to follow the system extensively and use this thesaurus for each individual line of the text. Others will dip in and out of the process, using it when they want to revitalise a specific objective or when they are rehearsing a particularly problematic scene.

The thesaurus can be used in two ways:

Alphabetical Thesaurus

If you know what action you are playing to achieve your objective in a given circumstance but want to try something else, then simply look up the verb you are playing in the main alphabetical thesaurus. You will be offered other choices of verbs which are all related. You can then begin a journey of cross-referencing that takes you through hundreds of potential choices.

Emotional Groups

If you have not decided what action you are playing, then turn to the Emotional Groups which follow the alphabetical thesaurus.

• Your first navigational choice is to decide what your character is trying to do to the other in the simplest terms. There is a choice of three directions. Is your character NURTURING, USING, or DAMAGING the other character/s? Make an instinctive choice, choose one category and turn to the page indicated.

• Each of the original choices will have led you to three more groups of words. For example, if you've chosen NURTURING words, you now have to decide whether this nurturing is LOVING, ENCOURAGING or SUPPORTING. Stay instinctive. Then once again turn to the appropriate page. If you've chosen a USING word, this will lead you to three other umbrella choices belonging to that word, i.e. one can 'use' someone, broadly speaking, in three different ways: by employing DISTURBING words, DECEIVING words, or MANIPULATING words. And finally, if you've decided you are using a DAMAGING word, then the options are subdivided into DISCOURAGING words, HARMING words, and DESTROYING words.

• If, for example, you choose LOVING, you will now be looking at a list of 'loving' verbs. The list is in simple alphabetical order. Choose your word, allow yourself a little poetry. Each word has its own place in the main alphabetical thesaurus. Look the word up. The list of alternatives alongside each word offers further creative options for investigation.

Most verbs vary in meaning according to their context. Some of the verbs from the thesaurus will not feature at all amongst the Emotional Groups, others will repeat themselves in more than one section. Compiling a definitive list is impossible. The emotional grouping is a subjective starting point designed for instant access to the subtext and a shortcut into the thesaurus. You can create your own emotional groupings according to your taste and definition.

Sample Scenes

In the following examples, the text is offered 'clean' followed by three alternative playings of that scene, with the different actions offered in brackets before each line of text. Try to ascertain for yourself what the objective for each character is, working directly from the specific choices made.

You may, of course, come up with a completely different set of choices from those suggested here. The variety of examples should illustrate how Actioning is applicable to texts from all dramatic genres.

SHAKESPEARE/CLASSICAL DRAMA

Twelfth Night
by Shakespeare (Act 1 Scene 5)

OLIVIA Whence came you, sir?

VIOLA I can say little more than I have studied, and that question's out of my part. Good gentle one, give me modest assurance, if you be the lady of the house, that I may proceed in my speech.

OLIVIA Are you are a comedian?

VIOLA No, my profound heart. And yet by the very fangs of malice, I swear I am not that I play. Are you the lady of the house?

OLIVIA If I do not usurp myself, I am.

So, according to the actors' objectives, one interpretation could be:

OLIVIA (Analyse) Whence came you, sir?

VIOLA (Tantalise) I can say little more than I have studied, and that question's out of

my part. (Hearten) Good gentle one, give
me modest assurance, if you be the lady of
the house, that I may proceed in my speech.

OLIVIA (Subjugate) Are you a comedian?

VIOLA (Sweeten) No, my profound heart.
(Stimulate) And yet by the very fangs of
malice, I swear I am not that I play. (Tease)
Are you the lady of the house?

OLIVIA (Humiliate) If I do not usurp myself,
I am.

Another interpretation:

OLIVIA (Captivate) Whence came you, sir?

VIOLA (Quieten) I can say little more than
I have studied, and that question's out of
my part. (Reproach) Good gentle one, give
me modest assurance, if you be the lady of
the house, that I may proceed in my speech.

OLIVIA (Mystify) Are you a comedian?

VIOLA (Reject) No, my profound heart.
(Estrange) And yet by the very fangs of
malice, I swear I am not that I play.
(Reprimand) Are you the lady of the house?

OLIVIA (Stimulate) If I do not usurp myself,
I am.

Or:

OLIVIA (Examine) Whence came you, sir?

VIOLA (Appease) I can say little more than
I have studied, and that question's out of
my part. (Caution) Good gentle one, give
me modest assurance, if you be the lady of
the house, that I may proceed in my speech.

OLIVIA (Malign) Are you a comedian?

VIOLA (Rebuff) No, my profound heart.
(Mellow) And yet by the very fangs of malice,

I swear I am not that I play. (Praise) Are
you the lady of the house?

OLIVIA (Unbalance) If I do not usurp myself,
I am.

PANTOMIME/COMEDY

Actioning works with any text, even with the
simplest and most formulaic form of writing,
like pantomime. Indeed, the technique is
especially useful for the actor performing a
play without, on first appearance, depth or
subtext. Actioning can bring precision and
truth to even the most apparently banal role.

The technique also helps to revitalise an actor
in a long run of a show – like a pantomime –
that might be playing three times a day and
might otherwise grow stale. The actor can
consciously play around with choices made in
the rehearsal room all those months ago.

Snow White and the Seven Dwarfs
by Julian Woolford and Marina Caldarone

RED QUEEN Muddles! Where have you been?

MUDDLES Have we met somewhere before?

RED QUEEN You've worked for me for eight
years.

MUDDLES I thought your face looked familiar.
Where have you been?

RED QUEEN What do you mean where have
I been? I sent you out two days ago to buy
me some nail varnish. Anyone would think
you'd been to Glasgow and back. Where've
you been?

MUDDLES Glasgow and back.

RED QUEEN What?

MUDDLES I can explain…

One version of choices might read:

RED QUEEN (Attack) Muddles! (Reprove) Where have you been?

MUDDLES (Avoid) Have we met somewhere before?

RED QUEEN (Challenge) You've worked for me for eight years.

MUDDLES (Reduce) I thought your face looked familiar. (Consider) Where have you been?

RED QUEEN (Accost) What do you mean, where have I been? (Remind) I sent you out two days ago to buy me some nail varnish. (Abuse) Anyone would think you'd been to Glasgow and back. (Assault) Where've you been?

MUDDLES (Battle) Glasgow and back.

RED QUEEN (Demoralise) What?

MUDDLES (Engage) I can explain…

Or:

RED QUEEN (Judge) Muddles! (Challenge) Where have you been?

MUDDLES (Congratulate) Have we met somewhere before?

RED QUEEN (Favour) You've worked for me for eight years.

MUDDLES (Applaud) I thought your face looked familiar. (Please) Where have you been?

RED QUEEN (Flatten) What do you mean, where have I been? (Coax) I sent you out two days ago to buy me some nail varnish. (Flatter) Anyone would think you'd been to Glasgow and back. (Pet) Where've you been?

MUDDLES (Trump) Glasgow and back.

RED QUEEN (Strike) What?

MUDDLES (Delight) I can explain…

Or:

RED QUEEN (Revere) Muddles! (Test) Where have you been?

MUDDLES (Dismiss) Have we met somewhere before?

RED QUEEN (Confront) You've worked for me for eight years.

MUDDLES (Befuddle) I thought your face looked familiar. (Patronise) Where have you been?

RED QUEEN (Hypnotise) What do you mean, where have I been? (Beguile) I sent you out two days ago to buy me some nail varnish. (Fascinate) Anyone would think you'd been to Glasgow and back. (Inflame) Where've you been?

MUDDLES (Obliterate) Glasgow and back.

RED QUEEN (Control) What?

MUDDLES (Agitate) I can explain…

CONTEMPORARY DRAMA

Dead Funny

by Terry Johnson (*the opening scene of the play*)

Eleanor sits motionless. On the floor scattered toys and the torso, its organs spilled. Richard, her husband, enters.

RICHARD One night only. Wimbledon Theatre. Sunday night. Norman Wisdom. Norman Wisdom.

ELEANOR Lucky Wimbledon.

RICHARD One night only.

ELEANOR Might have been a whole week.

RICHARD Mr Grimsdale!

ELEANOR You got a ticket?

RICHARD I got twelve.

ELEANOR Handy. When you fall asleep you can stretch out.

RICHARD Don't laugh at me, cause I'm a fool.

One interpretation:

RICHARD (Caution) One night only. (Warn) Wimbledon Theatre. (Discourage) Sunday night. (Dampen) Norman Wisdom. (Discourage) Norman Wisdom.

ELEANOR (Enliven) Lucky Wimbledon.

RICHARD (Dismiss) One night only.

ELEANOR (Delight) Might have been a whole week.

RICHARD (Demotivate) Mr Grimsdale!

ELEANOR (Probe) You got a ticket?

RICHARD (Amuse) I got twelve.

ELEANOR (Top) Handy. (Poke) When you fall asleep you can stretch out.

RICHARD (Entertain) Don't laugh at me cause I'm a fool.

Or:

RICHARD (Awaken) One night only. (Arouse) Wimbledon Theatre. (Stimulate) Sunday night. (Surprise) Norman Wisdom. (Excite) Norman Wisdom.

ELEANOR (Flick) Lucky Wimbledon.

RICHARD (Accuse) One night only.

ELEANOR (Knock) Might have been a whole week.

RICHARD (Shock) Mr Grimsdale!

ELEANOR (Applaud) You got a ticket?

RICHARD (Impress) I got twelve.

ELEANOR (Stroke) Handy. (Belittle) When you fall asleep you can stretch out.

RICHARD (Slap) Don't laugh at me cause I'm a
      fool.

Or:

RICHARD (Beseech) One night only. (Bewitch)
      Wimbledon Theatre. (Seduce) Sunday
      night. (Engross) Norman Wisdom.
      (Fascinate) Norman Wisdom.

ELEANOR (Deflect) Lucky Wimbledon.

RICHARD (Arouse) One night only.

ELEANOR (Tease) Might have been a whole
      week.

RICHARD (Pity) Mr Grimsdale!

ELEANOR (Torment) You got a ticket?

RICHARD (Block) I got twelve.

ELEANOR (Patronise) Handy. (Wound) When
      you fall asleep you can stretch out.

RICHARD (Shame) Don't laugh at me cause
      I'm a fool.

RADIO/TV COMMERCIAL VOICE-OVERS

As any actor knows, commercials and voice-
overs form an expanding sector of the job
market, and a very satisfying, and at times
lucrative, sector at that. The casting process
for this work is difficult to define and can be
a hit-and-miss business; often, for example,
the casting director is looking for a 'sound' to
sell the product. Since you can't act a 'sound',
it is important to ascertain what is required
from the script you will have been given to
read. You can then action the text to bring
what can be very artificial to life.

Take this text advertising a shopping centre.
It can be read a number of ways according to
choices made. Always have a very concrete idea

of the audience you are talking to – and let it always be an audience of one.

'You've never seen anything like this before. That's because nothing like this has ever been built before. So whatever you think shopping centres are like, you'd better think again. Silverwater. It's an experience to savour.'

You might be given some direction; you might not. Get as much information as you can and then play around. So, if you're asked to convey a seductive quality and your objective is to seduce the listener, you can play:

'1) You've never seen anything like this before. 2) That's because nothing like this has ever been built before. 3) So whatever you think shopping centres are like, you'd better think again. 4) Silverwater. 5) It's an experience to savour.'

1) Entice
2) Lure
3) Tempt
4) Delight
5) Bribe

All these actions are listed in the thesaurus under the word *seduce*. So, without coming out of that word, there are many ways to play these sentences without being repetitive or boring. You might equally go to another related word and find other alternatives that are less obviously seductive. The choice is there for you.

Thanks

The authors would like to thank Susan Angel, Kellie Bright, Emma Burnell, Lisa Carter, Beth Cordingly, Oliver Cotton, Kevin Francis, Jon Garside, Peter Guinness, Clifford Milner, Neil Pearson, Adrian Reed, Mark Scollan, Wanjiku and Murray Shelmerdine, Max Stafford-Clark, James Wilson, Julian Woolford and all their friends and family for their support and patience.

Acknowledgements

The publisher gratefully acknowledges permission to quote from the following:

Dead Funny by Terry Johnson, published by Methuen Publishing Limited.

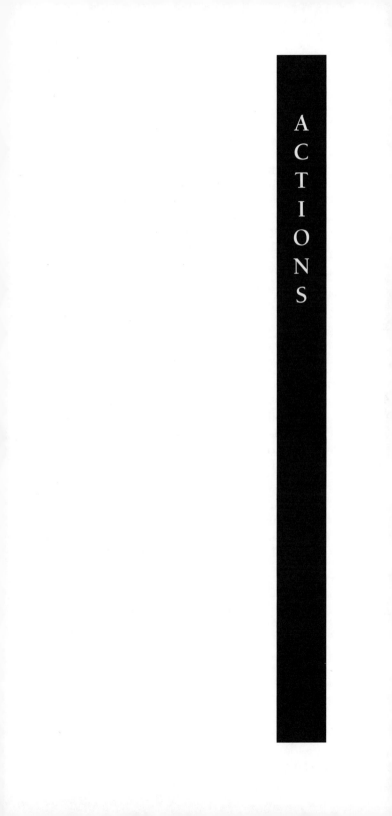

ACTIONS

Note

• This is a list of transitive verbs primarily for actors, directors and practitioners. It is not necessarily for academic reference, nor is it technically watertight. Language is subjective and there is a certain poetic licence in the lists which follow. However, all of the words can be 'played' by actors in performance.

• (PL) after an entry indicates where an action works best when played to more than one person. For example, *Assemble*, *Separate*, *Unite*.

• 1, 2, 3 after an entry indicates where more than one meaning can be attributed to that action.

• In a few instances, whilst X = Y, it does not always follow that Y = X. For example, *Conquer* is listed an action under the main entry *Butcher*, but the reverse does not work sufficiently well.

• This list is the first of its kind and should evolve and develop as used. Add any actions that you may feel are missing; suggestions for future editions would be gratefully received and should be addressed to the publisher.

**One thought – One sentence
One breath – One action**

Abandon   Desert, Discard, Ditch, Drop, Dump,
Forsake, Jilt, Leave, Reject, Relinquish,
Renounce, Shun, Snub, Surrender

Abduct   Capture, Entrap, Kidnap, Pluck,
Seize, Snatch

Abet   Advocate, Aid, Assist, Back, Boost,
Condone, Encourage, Endorse, Favour,
Forward, Foster, Further, Goad, Help,
Patronise, Promote, Provoke, Second,
Strengthen, Succour, Support

Abide   Bear, Endure, Obey, Stomach, Suffer,
Tolerate

Abjure   Discard, Renounce

Abolish   Annihilate, Destroy, Dismiss,
Eradicate, Nullify

Abridge   Condense, Encapsulate

Absolve   Acquit, Clear, Discharge, Exculpate,
Exempt, Exonerate, Forgive, Liberate,
Pardon, Purge, Purify, Redeem, Release,
Vindicate

Absorb   Consume, Digest, Envelop,
Incorporate, Process

Abuse   Assail, Attack, Berate, Blemish, Brutalise,
Censure, Curse, Damage, Decry, Defame,
Deprave, Deprecate, Disparage, Exploit,
Harangue, Harm, Hurt, Impair, Impugn,
Injure, Insult, Jeer, Knock, Malign, Maltreat,
Manhandle, Mar, Misemploy, Mistreat,
Misuse, Molest, Objurgate, Persecute,
Pervert, Rebuke, Revile, Ruin, Slander,
Torture, Use, Vilify, Violate, Wrong

Accelerate   Hasten, Hurry, Quicken, Spur,
Stimulate

Accept   Acknowledge, Admit, Adopt,
Approve, Condone, Embrace, Espouse,
Permit, Receive, Welcome

Access   Reach

Acclaim   Applaud, Approve, Cheer,
Commend, Exalt, Glorify, Hail, Honour,
Laud, Praise, Welcome

Acclimatise   Adapt, Adjust, Season

Accommodate, 1   Adapt, Adjust, Customise

Accommodate, 2   Contain, Foster, House,
Lodge, Place, Shelter

Accommodate, 3   Aid, Equip, Favour, Oblige

Accompany   Attend, Chaperone, Escort,
Follow, Lead, Track

Accost   Attack, Confront, Impugn

Accuse   Arraign, Blame, Challenge, Charge, Cite,
Defame, Denounce, Disparage, Expose,
Impeach, Indict, Incriminate, Prosecute

Accustom   Acquaint, Condition, Familiarise,
Habituate, Season

Acknowledge   Accept, Address, Admit,
Befriend, Greet, Hail, Notice, Receive,
Recognise, Tribute

Acquaint   Accustom, Advise, Appraise,
Befriend, Enlighten, Familiarise, Inform

Acquire   Attain

Acquit   Absolve, Clear, Deliver, Discharge,
Disencumber, Exempt, Exonerate,
Excuse, Forgive, Liberate, Pardon,
Release, Vindicate

Activate   Animate, Arouse, Awaken, Cue,
Deploy, Electrify, Energise, Enliven,
Galvanise, Generate, Impel, Initiate,
Inspirit, Instigate, Invigorate, Mobilise,
Motivate, Prompt, Rouse, Stimulate, Stir,
Trigger, Vitalise, Waken

Adapt   Acclimatise, Accommodate, Alter,
Amend, Change, Convert, Emend,
Prepare, Remodel, Shape, Tailor

Addle   Agitate, Befuddle, Confuse, Distract,
Dizzy

Address   Acknowledge, Approach, Greet,
Hail, Invoke, Name

4

Adjudicate Arbitrate, Judge, Mediate, Referee, Umpire

Adjure Command

Adjust Acclimatise, Convert

Admire Deify, Esteem, Honour, Idolise, Laud, Praise, Respect, Revere, Venerate

Admit Accept, Acknowledge, Adulate, Embrace, Encompass, Initiate, Involve, Permit, Recognise, Receive

Admonish Advise, Caution, Rebuke, Reprimand, Reprove, Reproach, Warn

Adopt Accept, Appropriate, Embrace, Espouse, Receive, Welcome

Adore Admire, Adulate, Cherish, Deify, Enshrine, Exalt, Idolise, Revere, Treasure, Venerate, Worship

Adorn Beautify, Bedeck, Crown, Deck, Decorate, Distinguish, Emblazon, Enrich, Festoon, Grace, Idolise, Ornament

Adulate Admire, Adore, Beatify, Cherish, Deify, Enshrine, Exalt, Idolise, Laud, Revere, Treasure, Venerate, Worship

Adulterate Bastardise, Bowdlerise, Contaminate, Corrupt, Debase, Devalue, Dilute, Dirty, Doctor, Pollute, Taint, Weaken

Advise Acquaint, Admonish, Alert, Appraise, Apprise, Caution, Counsel, Dissuade, Doctor, Educate, Encourage, Enlighten, Guide, Inform, Instruct, Notify, Prompt, Teach, Warn

Advocate Abet, Aid, Approve, Back, Boost, Champion, Encourage, Endorse, Favour, Forward, Further, Patronise

Affect Afflict, Alter, Change, Disturb, Influence, Interest, Modify, Move, Stir, Sway

Affirm Approve, Authorise, Aver, Back, Certify, Champion, Confirm, Endorse, Favour, Ratify, Recommend, Sanction, Support

Affix   Anchor, Fix, Pin, Secure, Wedge

Afflict   Affect, Bedevil, Bother, Curse, Distress, Hurt, Molest, Oppress, Persecute, Punish, Trouble

Affright   Alarm, Frighten, Horrify, Menace, Scare, Shock, Terrify, Terrorise

Affront   Charge, Degrade, Insult, Outrage, Provoke, Slander, Slight

Aggrandise   Boost, Dignify, Distend, Elevate, Ennoble, Exalt, Glorify, Honour, Inflate, Promote, Raise, Swell, Upgrade

Aggravate   Annoy, Antagonise, Bait, Bedevil, Bother, Embitter, Enrage, Exacerbate, Exasperate, Fret, Frustrate, Harass, Hassle, Hector, Hurt, Impair, Inflame, Irk, Irritate, Maltreat, Nark, Needle, Nettle, Pester, Provoke, Rankle, Rile, Tease, Torment, Vex

Aggrieve   Displease, Hurt

Agitate   Addle, Alarm, Arouse, Churn, Confuse, Derange, Disconcert, Distress, Disturb, Disquiet, Dizzy, Fan, Faze, Fluster, Fret, Generate, Harass, Hassle, Impel, Incite, Inflame, Jumble, Panic, Perturb, Press, Rattle, Rouse, Ruffle, Shake, Shock, Startle, Stimulate, Stir, Trouble, Unnerve, Unsettle, Upset, Vex, Worry

Aid   Abet, Accommodate, Advocate, Assist, Back, Befriend, Bolster, Boost, Comfort, Cultivate, Ease, Encourage, Favour, Forward, Foster, Further, Help, Improve, Nurse, Refresh, Relieve, Remedy, Restore, Revive, Save, Serve, Strengthen, Succour, Support, Teach, Tutor

Alarm   Affright, Agitate, Alert, Distress, Disturb, Frighten, Horrify, Menace, Panic, Perturb, Petrify, Scare, Signal, Startle, Terrify, Terrorise, Threaten, Unnerve, Warn

Alert Advise, Alarm, Awaken, Caution, Forewarn, Notify, Signal, Warn

Alienate Disillusion, Distance, Embitter, Envenom, Poison, Sour

Align Compose, Harmonise

Allay Alleviate, Appease, Assuage, Calm, Comfort, Disburden, Ease, Lighten, Lull, Pacify, Placate, Quieten, Relax, Relieve, Settle, Soothe, Still, Temper, Tranquillise

Alleviate Allay, Appease, Assuage, Calm, Comfort, Disburden, Disencumber, Ease, Help, Lessen, Lighten, Quieten, Relax, Relieve, Remedy, Restore, Soothe, Still, Sweeten, Tranquillise

Allocate Place

Allure Arrest, Attract, Beckon, Bewitch, Captivate, Charm, Coax, Decoy, Delight, Enamour, Enchant, Engage, Entice, Fascinate, Induce, Inveigle, Lure, Persuade, Seduce, Tempt, Win

Ally Befriend, Join

Alter Adapt, Affect, Amend, Change, Convert, Modify, Reform, Remodel, Reshape, Transform, Turn

Amaze Astonish, Astound, Baffle, Bewilder, Confound, Daze, Dazzle, Dumbfound, Electrify, Flabbergast, Floor, Impress, Jolt, Mystify, Shock, Stagger, Startle, Stimulate, Stir, Stun, Stupefy, Surprise

Ambush Endanger, Ensnare, Surprise, Trap

Amend Alter, Better, Change, Correct, Emend, Fix, Improve, Mend, Modify, Reform

Amputate Axe, Cut, Remove, Sever

Amuse Beguile, Charm, Cheer, Delight, Enliven, Entertain, Gladden, Gratify, Humour, Please, Regale, Tickle

Anaesthetise Deactivate, Deaden, Dull, Numb, Paralyse, Petrify

Analyse   Assess, Appraise, Consider, Criticise,
        Deconstruct, Dissect, Estimate, Evaluate,
        Examine, Investigate, Judge, Scrutinise,
        Study

Anathematise   Curse, Damn, Deactivate,
        Deaden, Denounce

Anchor   Affix, Fix, Root, Secure, Stabilise

Animate   Activate, Arouse, Awaken, Boost,
        Brighten, Cheer, Elate, Electrify, Elevate,
        Embolden, Encourage, Enliven, Energise,
        Excite, Exhilarate, Fire, Galvanise,
        Hearten, Impel, Incite, Inflame, Inspire,
        Inspirit, Invigorate, Mobilise, Motivate,
        Move, Nerve, Raise, Rally, Revive, Rouse,
        Shock, Spark, Spur, Stimulate, Thrill,
        Urge, Uplift, Vitalise, Vivify, Waken,
        Warm

Annihilate   Abolish, Cancel, Demolish,
        Destroy, Eliminate, Eradicate, Excise,
        Execute, Expunge, Exterminate, Extin-
        guish, Extirpate, Finish, Kill, Massacre,
        Murder, Negate, Nullify, Obliterate, Raze,
        Slaughter, Slay, Terminate

Annoy   Aggravate, Antagonise, Badger, Bait,
        Bedevil, Bother, Bug, Displease, Distress,
        Disturb, Exasperate, Fret, Goad, Harass,
        Harry, Hassle, Hinder, Irk, Irritate,
        Madden, Nag, Nark, Needle, Nettle,
        Niggle, Peeve, Pester, Plague, Provoke,
        Rattle, Rile, Ruffle, Trouble, Vex, Weary,
        Worry

Anoint   Bless, Consecrate, Hallow, Ordain,
        Sanctify

Antagonise   Aggravate, Annoy, Exasperate,
        Harass, Hassle, Incense, Insult, Irk,
        Irritate, Nark, Outrage, Provoke, Repel

Ape   Copy, Echo, Imitate, Mirror, Parrot,
        Reflect

Appall   Disgust, Dismay, Frighten, Horrify,
        Scandalise, Shock, Sicken

Appease   Allay, Alleviate, Assuage, Calm, Comfort, Conciliate, Content, Disburden, Ease, Hush, Indulge, Mollify, Pacify, Placate, Propitiate, Quieten, Reconcile, Relax, Relieve, Satisfy, Soothe, Still, Sweeten, Tranquillise

Applaud   Acclaim, Approve, Cheer, Commend, Congratulate, Encourage, Extol, Glorify, Hail, Honour, Laud, Praise, Welcome

Appoint   Assign, Authorise, Commission, Delegate, Designate, Elect, Employ, Engage, Enlist, Enrol, Nominate, Ordain, Pick, Select

Appraise   Acquaint, Advise, Analyse, Assess, Audition, Criticise, Estimate, Evaluate, Gauge, Judge, Measure, Test, Try, Value, Vet

Apprehend, 1   Arrest, Stop

Apprehend, 2   Consider, Recognise

Apprise   Advise, Counsel, Edify, Educate, Enlighten, Inform, Instruct, Teach, Tutor

Approach   Address, Broach, Greet

Appropriate   Adopt, Claim, Conquer, Devour, Filch, Hog, Misuse, Own, Plunder, Purloin, Reclaim, Requisition, Steal

Approve   Accept, Acclaim, Advocate, Affirm, Applaud, Authorise, Champion, Commend, Condone, Confirm, Endorse, Favour, Permit, Ratify, Sanction

Arbitrate   Adjudicate, Judge, Mediate, Referee, Umpire

Arm   Brace, Defend, Empower, Equip, Interest, Prepare, Prime, Protect, Strengthen

Arouse   Activate, Agitate, Animate, Awaken, Encourage, Energise, Enkindle, Enliven, Excite, Fan, Fire, Galvanise, Generate, Goad, Impassion, Incite, Inflame, Inspire,

9

Interest, Intoxicate, Intrigue, Invigorate,
Kindle, Move, Prod, Provoke, Revive,
Rouse, Spark, Spur, Stimulate, Stir, Thrill,
Titillate, Vitalise, Vivify, Waken, Warm

Arraign   Accuse, Blame, Charge, Denounce,
Indict

Arrest, 1   Allure, Assail, Captivate, Charm,
Enamour, Enchant, Engage, Engross,
Engulf, Fascinate, Impress

Arrest, 2   Apprehend, Block, Capture, Catch,
Convict, Hold, Nab, Nail, Nick,
Obstruct, Restrain, Seize, Suppress

Arrest 3   Apprehend, Freeze, Halt,
Immobilise, Numb, Paralyse, Stop, Stun

Assail   Abuse, Arrest, Assault, Attack,
Bombard, Charge, Impugn, Invade, Pelt,
Permeate, Torment

Assault   Assail, Attack, Batter, Bombard, Box,
Bruise, Challenge, Charge, Combat,
Damage, Debauch, Fight, Harm, Hit,
Impugn, Invade, Mob, Molest, Mug,
Punch, Raid, Rape, Savage, Storm, Strike,
Violate

Assemble (PL)   Congregate, Rally

Assess   Analyse, Appraise, Audition,
Calculate, Criticise, Estimate, Evaluate,
Gauge, Judge, Measure, Test, Value

Assign   Appoint, Authorise, Consign,
Delegate, Nominate

Assist   Abet, Aid, Back, Bolster, Cultivate,
Encourage, Expedite, Favour, Forward,
Further, Help, Improve, Nurse, Promote,
Relieve, Restore, Save, Second, Serve,
Spur, Strengthen, Succour, Support,
Sustain, Tutor

Assuage   Allay, Alleviate, Appease, Calm,
Comfort, Console, Cradle, Disburden,
Ease, Lighten, Lull, Mollify, Pacify,
Placate, Quieten, Relax, Relieve, Satisfy,
Soothe, Still, Temper, Tranquillise

Assure   Convince, Embolden, Encourage, Hearten, Inspirit, Persuade, Reassure, Secure, Settle, Stabilise, Warrant

Astonish   Amaze, Astound, Bewilder, Confound, Daze, Dazzle, Dumbfound, Electrify, Excite, Flabbergast, Floor, Jolt, Mystify, Shock, Stagger, Startle, Stimulate, Stun, Stupefy, Surprise

Astound   Amaze, Astonish, Baffle, Bewilder, Confound, Daze, Dumbfound, Flabbergast, Floor, Shock, Stagger, Stir, Strike, Stun, Stupefy, Surprise

Attack   Abuse, Accost, Assail, Assault, Battle, Berate, Blast, Bombard, Box, Censure, Challenge, Charge, Combat, Criticise, Denounce, Dispraise, Fight, Hawk, Impugn, Indict, Infest, Invade, Knock, Lash, Malign, Maul, Mug, Persecute, Raid, Ram, Savage, Slander, Storm, Strike, Tackle, Vilify

Attain   Acquire, Procure, Reach, Secure, Win

Attend   Accompany, Chaperone, Escort, Serve, Usher

Attire   Clothe, Dress

Attract   Allure, Beckon, Bewitch, Captivate, Charm, Delight, Enamour, Enchant, Endear, Engage, Entice, Fascinate, Impress, Induce, Intrigue, Invite, Lure, Magnetise, Pull, Rivet, Seduce, Tempt, Titillate, Win

Auction   Prostitute, Sell

Audition   Appraise, Assess, Test

Augment   Bolster, Boost, Elevate, Encourage, Enlarge, Feed, Fuel, Heighten, Inflate, Reinforce, Strengthen, Sustain, Swell

Authorise   Affirm, Approve, Back, Commission, Confirm, Delegate, Empower, Enable, Endorse, Entitle, Favour, Legitimise, License, Permit, Qualify, Ratify, Sanction, Support, Warrant

Avenge   Punish

Aver   Affirm, Back, Favour, Recommend,
    Support

Avert   Deflect, Divert, Parry

Avoid   Deflect, Disregard, Dodge, Elude,
    Escape, Evade, Neglect, Ostracise, Parry,
    Shirk, Shun, Sidestep

Awaken   Activate, Alert, Animate, Arouse,
    Enkindle, Enliven, Excite, Fire,
    Galvanise, Generate, Ignite, Incite,
    Inflame, Inspire, Kindle, Provoke,
    Revive, Rouse, Sober, Spur, Stimulate,
    Stir, Vitalise, Vivify, Waken

Award   Bequeath, Bestow, Endow, Enrich,
    Furnish, Grant, Honour, Prize, Reward,
    Will

Axe   Amputate, Chop

Back   Abet, Advocate, Affirm, Aid, Assist,
Authorise, Aver, Champion, Commend,
Condone, Confirm, Cultivate, Encourage,
Endorse, Espouse, Favour, Help,
Promote, Ratify, Recommend, Sanction,
Second, Sponsor, Succour, Support,
Sustain, Uphold, Warrant

Badger   Annoy, Besiege, Bug, Bully, Disturb,
Fret, Goad, Harass, Harry, Hassle, Heckle,
Hector, Hound, Nag, Persecute, Pester,
Plague, Taunt, Tease, Trouble, Torment,
Vex, Worry

Baffle   Amaze, Bamboozle, Befuddle,
Bewilder, Confuse, Confound, Daze,
Disconcert, Dumbfound, Elude, Faze,
Floor, Flummox, Foil, Forestall,
Frustrate, Mystify, Outwit, Perplex,
Puzzle, Stump

Bait   Aggravate, Annoy, Bother, Decoy, Entrap,
Harass, Hassle, Heckle, Hound, Irritate,
Irk, Jeer, Lure, Nark, Needle, Persecute,
Pester, Provoke, Taunt, Tease, Torment

Balance   Counteract, Equalise, Ground,
Level, Regulate, Settle, Stabilise, Steady

Bamboozle   Baffle, Confound, Confuse,
Deceive, Defraud, Delude, Dupe, Entrap,
Fool, Gull, Hoax, Hoodwink, Mystify,
Puzzle, Skin, Swindle, Trick

Ban   Bar, Banish, Block, Boycott, Censor,
Debar, Disallow, Disqualify, Exclude,
Forbid, Hamper, Impede, Indict, Interdict,
Outlaw, Prohibit, Restrict, Stop, Suppress

Bang   Bash, Bat, Beat, Belt, Bump, Burst,
Clobber, Cuff, Hammer, Hit, Knock,
Pound, Pummel, Slam, Slap, Smack,
Spank, Strike, Thump, Thwack, Whack

Banish   Ban, Boycott, Dismiss, Displace,
       Dispossess, Eject, Eliminate, Eradicate,
       Exclude, Exile, Expel, Fire, Interdict, Oust,
       Outlaw, Ostracise, Reject, Sack, Spurn

Baptise   Cleanse, Name

Bar   Ban, Barricade, Block, Boycott, Disallow,
       Exclude, Forbid, Hamper, Hinder,
       Impede, Interdict, Obstruct, Prohibit,
       Restrict, Stop

Barricade   Bar, Fortify, Obstruct, Protect,
       Secure

Bash   Bang, Batter, Beat, Hit, Punch, Slam

Bastardise   Adulterate, Bowdlerise, Corrupt

Bat   Bang, Hit, Punch, Rap, Slug, Smack,
       Strike, Swat, Thump, Wallop

Batter   Assault, Bash, Beat, Bombard, Break,
       Bruise, Clobber, Cuff, Crush, Dash,
       Demolish, Destroy, Hammer, Hit, Hurt,
       Injure, Lash, Maul, Pelt, Pound, Pummel,
       Ruin, Shatter, Slug, Smash, Smite, Sock,
       Strike, Thrash, Thump, Thwack, Trash,
       Wallop, Whack

Battle   Assault, Attack, Befuddle, Box,
       Challenge, Combat, Confront, Fight, Hit

Bear, 1   Carry, Convey, Harbour, Shoulder,
       Support, Sustain, Transport

Bear, 2   Abide, Endure, Stand, Stomach,
       Suffer, Support, Tolerate

Beat, 1   Bang, Bash, Batter, Belt, Break, Bruise,
       Cane, Chastise, Chin, Clobber, Clout,
       Conquer, Crush, Cudgel, Cuff, Deck, Defeat,
       Demolish, Flagellate, Flail, Flog, Floor,
       Hammer, Hit, Knock, Lash, Maul, Pelt, Pound,
       Pulverise, Pummel, Punch, Quash, Scourge,
       Shake, Slap, Slug, Smack, Sock, Spank, Strap,
       Strike, Swipe, Tan, Thump, Thwack, Thrash,
       Trample, Wallop, Whack, Whip

Beat, 2   Better, Defeat, Outdo, Outstrip,
       Outwit, Overwhelm, Surpass, Trounce,
       Vanquish

Beatify   Adulate, Deify, Exalt, Idolise,
   Immortalise, Revere, Sanctify, Venerate,
   Worship

Beautify   Adorn, Bedeck, Better, Deck,
   Decorate, Enrich, Festoon, Grace,
   Improve, Ornament

Beckon   Allure, Attract, Bid, Call, Draw, Entice,
   Invite, Lure, Pull, Signal, Summon

Bedeck   Adorn, Beautify, Deck, Decorate,
   Enrich, Festoon, Ornament

Bedevil   Afflict, Aggravate, Annoy, Confound,
   Distress, Frustrate, Harass, Harry, Hassle,
   Irk, Irritate, Pester, Plague, Trouble, Vex,
   Worry

Befoul   Poison, Pollute

Befriend   Acknowledge, Acquaint, Aid, Ally,
   Commend, Encourage, Favour, Help,
   Patronise, Support, Uphold

Befuddle   Addle, Battle, Bewilder, Cloud,
   Confound, Confuse, Disorientate,
   Dumbfound, Jumble, Muddle, Mystify,
   Perplex, Puzzle, Stump

Beg   Beseech, Entreat, Implore, Importune,
   Parry, Solicit

Beget   Generate, Incite, Provoke

Beguile   Amuse, Belittle, Bewitch, Cajole,
   Captivate, Charm, Cheat, Coax, Con,
   Court, Deceive, Defraud, Delight, Dupe,
   Enamour, Enchant, Engage, Enrapture,
   Enthrall, Entice, Entrance, Fascinate,
   Flatter, Fool, Hoodwink, Hypnotise,
   Induce, Inveigle, Kid, Lure, Mesmerise,
   Mislead, Seduce, Spellbind, Trick

Behold   Conjure

Belittle   Beguile, Cheapen, Decry, Demean,
   Discredit, Dispraise, Humiliate, Knock,
   Patronise

Belt   Bang, Beat, Clobber, Cuff, Flog,
   Hammer, Hit, Slug, Smite, Sock, Strip,
   Wallop, Whack

Bemuse   Bewilder, Confuse, Daze, Distract,
    Flummox, Fuddle, Muddle, Perplex,
    Preoccupy, Stun, Stupefy

Bend   Break, Contort, Distort, Pervert, Twist,
    Warp

Benumb   Daze, Deactivate, Deaden,
    Inactivate, Paralyse

Bequeath   Award

Berate   Abuse, Attack, Castigate, Censure,
    Chastise, Denigrate, Denounce, Impugn,
    Knock, Lambast, Rebuke, Reprehend,
    Reprimand, Reproach, Scold, Vilify

Bereave   Afflict, Deprive, Dispossess

Beseech   Beg, Entreat, Implore, Solicit

Besiege   Badger, Block, Bother, Confine,
    Encircle, Encompass, Harass, Harry,
    Hassle, Hound, Nag, Pester, Plague, Sap,
    Swamp, Surround

Besmear   Contaminate, Defile, Dirty, Foul,
    Pollute, Smear, Soil, Stain, Taint

Bestir   Rouse, Wake

Bestow   Award

Betray   Deceive, Desert, Discard, Forsake, Jilt,
    Reject

Betroth   Bind, Commit, Engage

Better, 1   Amend, Beautify, Cultivate, Dignify,
    Improve, Mend, Reform, Sophisticate

Better, 2   Beat, Defeat, Outdo, Outsmart,
    Outstrip, Surpass, Top

Bewilder   Amaze, Astonish, Astound, Baffle,
    Befuddle, Bemuse, Confuse, Confound,
    Daze, Faze, Floor, Flummox, Mystify,
    Perplex, Puzzle, Shock, Stump, Stun,
    Stupefy, Surprise

Bewitch   Allure, Attract, Beguile, Captivate,
    Catch, Charm, Curse, Delight, Enamour,
    Enchant, Enrapture, Enthrall, Entrance,
    Fascinate, Hypnotise, Mesmerise,
    Spellbind, Transport

Bid   Beckon, Command

16

Bind, 1 (PL)   Betroth, Cement, Chain,
  Commit, Engage, Fetter, Fix, Restrain,
  Restrict, Secure, Shackle, Tie

Bind, 2   Captivate, Charm, Endear, Engage

Bind, 3   Chain, Confine, Constrain,
  Encumber, Enslave, Fetter, Fix, Hold,
  Pinion, Subjugate, Yoke

Birch   Cane, Flagellate, Flog, Strap, Tan,
  Whip

Bisect   Divide, Split, Sunder

Bite   Champ, Chew, Clamp, Crunch, Cut,
  Gnaw, Nip, Tear, Wound

Blacken   Damn, Decry, Defame, Defile,
  Denigrate, Dishonour, Impugn, Malign,
  Slander, Smear, Smirch, Stain, Taint,
  Tarnish, Traduce, Vilify

Blackmail   Bribe, Coerce, Compel, Fleece,
  Intimidate, Terrorise, Threaten

Blame   Accuse, Arraign, Censure, Charge,
  Condemn, Criticise, Disparage, Impeach,
  Incriminate, Indict, Reprehend,
  Reproach

Blast   Attack, Castigate, Censure, Criticise,
  Cuss, Demolish, Decry, Destroy, Fire,
  Flay, Impugn, Shatter

Blazon   Decorate, Honour

Blemish   Abuse, Corrupt, Damage, Deface,
  Impair, Mar, Scar, Taint, Vandalise

Bless   Anoint, Consecrate, Glorify, Hallow,
  Praise, Sanctify, Thank

Blight   Contaminate, Impair, Infect, Mar,
  Taint

Blind   Bluff, Daze, Dazzle, Deceive, Distract

Block   Arrest, Ban, Bar, Capture, Confound,
  Confront, Curb, Delay, Deter, Elude,
  Forestall, Frustrate, Gag, Halt, Hamper,
  Handicap, Hinder, Impede, Inhibit,
  Intercept, Interdict, Obstruct, Prohibit,
  Proscribe, Restrain, Restrict, Stop,
  Stump, Thwart

Bludgeon   Cudgel, Destroy, Flog, Lambast, Thrash

Bluff   Blind, Deceive, Defraud, Delude, Fool, Hoax, Misguide, Mislead

Bolster   Aid, Assist, Augment, Boost, Brace, Encourage, Feed, Fuel, Nurture, Reassure, Reinforce, Strengthen, Support, Sustain

Bombard   Assail, Assault, Attack, Batter, Besiege, Blast, Harass, Hound, Pelt, Pester

Bond (PL)   Bind, Cement, Fix, Fuse, Glue, Paste

Boost   Abet, Advocate, Aggrandise, Aid, Animate, Augment, Bolster, Brighten, Cheer, Compliment, Distend, Elate, Elevate, Encourage, Enhance, Exalt, Excite, Exhilarate, Expand, Favour, Forward, Foster, Further, Hearten, Heighten, Help, Improve, Inflate, Intensify, Invigorate, Lift, Nourish, Nurse, Promote, Raise, Reinforce, Reward, Rouse, Spur, Stimulate, Strengthen, Support, Swell, Toughen, Uplift, Urge

Boot   Eject, Kick

Bother   Afflict, Aggravate, Annoy, Bait, Besiege, Bug, Burden, Concern, Distract, Distress, Disturb, Faze, Fluster, Fret, Fuss, Harass, Hassle, Inconvenience, Perturb, Pester, Tease, Trouble, Unsettle, Upset, Worry

Bowdlerise   Adulterate, Bastardise, Corrupt

Box, 1   Assault, Attack, Battle, Challenge, Clobber, Cuff, Fight, Hit, Sock, Whack

Box, 2   Bind, Corner, Constrain, Pigeonhole, Trap

Boycott   Ban, Banish, Bar, Exclude, Exile, Ignore, Ostracise, Prohibit, Reject

Brace   Arm, Bolster, Reinforce, Strengthen, Support

Brainwash   Indoctrinate

Brand   Burn, Grade, Mark

Break, 1   Batter, Beat, Bend, Burst, Bust, Crack, Cripple, Crumble, Crush, Damage, Defeat, Demolish, Destroy, Disable, Disunite, Fracture, Fragment, Harm, Impoverish, Incapacitate, Injure, Pulverise, Reduce, Sever, Shatter, Smash, Snap, Splinter, Split, Strike, Tear, Warp, Wound

Break, 2   Demoralise, Dispirit, Enervate, Enfeeble, Subdue, Weaken

Bribe   Blackmail, Corrupt, Induce, Seduce, Tempt

Brief   Inform, Prepare, Prime

Brighten   Animate, Boost, Cheer, Elate, Elevate, Enliven, Excite, Exhilarate, Gladden, Hearten, Ignite, Inspire, Inspirit, Invigorate, Raise, Rouse, Stimulate, Uplift, Vitalise

Broach, 1   Approach, Tackle

Broach, 2   Penetrate, Pierce

Browbeat   Bully, Chide, Criticise, Harass, Hector, Henpeck, Nag, Pester, Scold, Torment

Bruise   Assault, Batter, Beat, Crush, Damage, Injure, Insult, Offend, Pulverise, Wound

Brush   Buff, Caress, Groom, Kiss, Stroke, Touch

Brutalise   Abuse, Bully, Bulldoze, Intimidate, Mistreat, Pressurise

Buff   Brush, Rub

Bug   Annoy, Badger, Bother, Fret, Harry, Hassle, Plague, Torment, Vex

Bulldoze   Brutalise, Bully, Demolish, Flatten, Pressurise, Raze, Squash

Bully   Badger, Browbeat, Brutalise, Bulldoze, Chide, Frighten, Harass, Hector, Henpeck, Hound, Intimidate, Menace, Nag, Oppress, Persecute, Pester, Repress, Terrorise, Threaten, Torment, Tyrannise, Victimise

B

Bump   Bang, Crowd, Elbow, Hustle, Jab,
         Jostle, Knock, Nudge, Push, Shock,
         Shoulder, Shove, Strike
Burden   Bother, Encumber, Hamper,
         Handicap, Hinder, Impede,
         Inconvenience, Obstruct, Oppress,
         Overload, Saddle, Trammel, Trouble,
         Weary
Burn   Brand, Immolate, Incinerate, Kindle
Burst   Bang, Break, Crack, Shatter, Split
Bury   Deluge, Drown, Submerge
Bust   Break
Butcher   Conquer, Exterminate, Kill, Mangle,
         Massacre, Mutilate, Slaughter, Slay
Butter   Flatter

Cage   Confine, Imprison, Incarcerate

Cajole   Beguile, Coax, Court, Entice, Flatter, Inveigle, Lure, Persuade, Pressure, Stoke, Tempt

Calculate   Assess, Estimate, Measure

Call   Beckon, Command, Evoke, Incite, Name, Summon

Calm   Allay, Alleviate, Appease, Assuage, Comfort, Compose, Disburden, Ease, Hush, Lessen, Lighten, Lull, Mollify, Pacify, Placate, Quell, Quieten, Relax, Rock, Sedate, Settle, Silence, Smooth, Sober, Soothe, Still, Temper, Tranquillise

Cancel   Annihilate, Destroy, Efface, Eradicate, Excise, Expunge, Extirpate, Invalidate, Obliterate, Raze, Rescind

Cane   Beat, Birch, Flagellate, Flog, Strap, Tan, Whip

Capacitate   Empower, Enfranchise

Captivate   Allure, Arrest, Attract, Beguile, Bewitch, Bind, Catch, Charm, Dazzle, Delight, Enamour, Enchant, Endear, Engage, Engross, Enrapture, Enthrall, Entrance, Excite, Fascinate, Fixate, Hypnotise, Intrigue, Mesmerise, Ravish, Rivet, Seize, Spellbind, Titillate, Win

Capture   Abduct, Arrest, Block, Catch, Clutch, Ensnare, Grab, Hijack, Hold, Kidnap, Nab, Nail, Net, Nick, Overmaster, Pluck, Snare, Snatch, Subjugate, Win

Caress   Brush, Cuddle, Embrace, Fondle, Hug, Kiss, Lick, Massage, Nuzzle, Pat, Paw, Pet, Rub, Stroke, Touch

Caricature   Imitate, Mimic, Parody, Satirise

Carry   Bear, Hold, Shoulder, Support, Transport

Castigate   Berate, Blast, Censure, Chasten,
        Chastise, Chide, Condemn, Criticise,
        Denounce, Flagellate, Flog, Lambast,
        Punish, Rebuke, Reprehend, Reprimand,
        Reproach, Reprove, Scold, Strap, Tan, Whip
Castrate   Disempower, Emasculate, Sterilise
Catch   Arrest, Bewitch, Captivate, Capture,
        Charm, Detect, Enchant, Enmesh,
        Ensnare, Entangle, Grab, Hook, Nail,
        Pluck, Snare, Snatch, Trap
Catechise   Cross-examine, Interrogate,
        Question, Quiz
Categorise   Compute, Confine, Class, Classify,
        Grade, Limit, Rank, Restrain, Restrict
Caution   Admonish, Advise, Alert, Counsel,
        Discourage, Dissuade, Reprove, Warn
Cement (PL)   Bind, Bond
Censor, 1   Emend, Sanitise
Censor, 2   Ban, Exclude, Obliterate, Prohibit,
        Restrain
Censure   Abuse, Attack, Blame, Berate, Blast,
        Castigate, Chastise, Condemn, Criticise,
        Decry, Denounce, Impugn, Knock, Lambast,
        Lecture, Rebuke, Reprimand, Reprove, Scold
Centre   Focus, Ground
Certify, 1   Affirm, Confirm, Qualify
Certify, 2   Section
Chain   Bind, Confine, Constrain, Constrict,
        Encumber, Enslave, Fetter, Fix, Hamper,
        Hold, Lock, Manacle, Pinion, Restrain,
        Restrict, Secure, Tie, Yoke
Challenge   Accuse, Assault, Attack, Battle, Box,
        Confront, Contest, Cross-examine, Dare,
        Defy, Embattle, Fight, Interrogate, Oppose,
        Question, Resist, Rival, Tackle, Threaten
Champion   Advocate, Affirm, Approve,
        Commend, Confirm, Back, Defend,
        Encourage, Favour, Forward, Further,
        Patronise, Promote, Push, Ratify, Second,
        Support, Warrant

Change   Adapt, Affect, Alter, Amend,
     Convert, Reform, Transform, Turn

Chaperone   Accompany, Attend, Escort,
     Protect, Safeguard, Shepherd

Charge, 1   Affront, Arraign, Assail, Assault,
     Attack, Blame, Mob, Ram, Strike

Charge, 2   Accuse, Command, Disparage, Fuel,
     Impeach, Incriminate, Indict, Prosecute

Charge, 3   Fuel, Revive

Charm   Allure, Amuse, Arrest, Attract,
     Beguile, Bewitch, Bind, Captivate, Catch,
     Court, Delight, Enamour, Enchant,
     Endear, Engage, Enthrall, Entrance,
     Enrapture, Fascinate, Flatter, Hypnotise,
     Intrigue, Inveigle, Mesmerise, Please,
     Ravish, Spellbind, Titillate, Win

Chase   Follow, Hunt, Pursue, Stalk, Track, Trail

Chasten   Castigate, Chastise, Discipline,
     Humble

Chastise   Beat, Berate, Castigate, Censure,
     Chasten, Chide, Correct, Discipline, Flog,
     Punish, Rebuke, Reprehend, Nag, Scold

Cheapen   Belittle, Debase, Degrade, Demean,
     Denigrate, Devalue, Discredit, Disparage,
     Dispirit, Lower

Cheat   Beguile, Con, Deceive, Defraud,
     Delude, Diddle, Dupe, Fleece, Fool, Gull,
     Hoax, Hoodwink, Outwit, Rob, Swindle,
     Trick, Wrong

Check, 1   Frisk, Vet

Check, 2   Control, Hinder, Stop

Cheer, 1   Amuse, Animate, Applaud, Boost,
     Brighten, Comfort, Console, Delight,
     Elate, Elevate, Embolden, Encourage,
     Enhearten, Enliven, Excite, Fire, Fortify,
     Gladden, Hearten, Inspire, Inspirit,
     Invigorate, Jolly, Lighten, Please, Rally,
     Reassure, Refresh, Revive, Rouse,
     Stimulate, Stir, Strengthen, Sustain,
     Tickle, Uplift, Vitalise, Warm

Cheer, 2   Acclaim, Applaud, Hail

Cherish   Adore, Adulate, Conserve, Enshrine,
       Immortalise, Nurture, Pet, Prize,
       Treasure, Value

Chide   Browbeat, Bully, Castigate, Chastise,
       Criticise, Curse, Harass, Hector, Henpeck,
       Intimidate, Lecture, Nag, Rebuff, Rebuke,
       Reprehend, Reprimand, Reproach,
       Reprove, Scold

Chill   Cool, Depress, Discourage, Dishearten,
       Numb

Chip   Dent, Nick, Notch

Choke   Constrict, Gag, Obstruct, Smother,
       Stifle, Strangle, Suffocate, Throttle

Choose   Designate, Elect, Nominate, Pick,
       Select

Chop   Axe, Cut, Hack, Slash

Chuck   Fling, Sling, Throw

Churn   Agitate, Stir

Circle   Circumscribe, Encircle, Enclose,
       Encompass, Enfold, Envelop, Surround

Circumscribe   Circle, Cover, Encircle,
       Enclose, Encompass, Enfold, Envelop,
       Hedge, Pen, Surround, Wrap

Civilise   Coach, Cultivate, Develop,
       Discipline, Edify, Educate, Enlighten,
       Improve, Inform, Instruct, Polish, Refine,
       School, Sophisticate, Teach, Train, Tutor

Claim   Appropriate, Own

Clasp   Clinch, Clutch, Embrace, Enfold,
       Envelop, Enwrap, Hold, Press, Seize,
       Squeeze, Swathe, Wrap

Class   Categorise, Classify, Grade, Label,
       Name, Rank, Rate, Value

Classify   Categorise, Class, Grade, Order,
       Rate, Rank, Tag, Value

Cleanse   Baptise, Purify, Rinse, Scrub, Wash

Clear, 1   Absolve, Acquit, Discharge,
       Disengage, Disentangle, Excuse,
       Exonerate, Free, Vindicate

Clear, 2 Disengage, Disentangle, Lighten, Relieve, Unblock, Unburden

Cleave, 1 Cut, Gash, Gouge, Hack, Lacerate, Slash, Slit, Smite, Split, Tear

Cleave, 2 (PL) Divide, Incise, Separate, Sever, Split, Sunder

Clinch Clasp, Embrace, Hug, Squeeze

Clip Clout, Hit, Smack

Clobber Bang, Batter, Beat, Belt, Box, Cuff, Hammer, Hit, Knock, Lambast, Slap, Slog, Smack, Sock, Strike, Wallop, Whack

Clog Block, Burden, Congest, Cramp, Encumber, Hamper, Handicap, Hinder, Impede, Obstruct, Oppress, Overload, Retard

Clothe Attire, Dress

Cloud, 1 Befuddle, Clothe, Confuse, Disorientate, Impair, Muddle

Cloud, 2 Dim, Extinguish, Obscure

Clout Beat, Clip, Hit, Smack

Clutch Capture, Clasp, Embrace, Grab, Grasp, Grip, Hold, Pluck, Seize, Snatch

Coach Civilise, Cultivate, Develop, Discipline, Drill, Edify, Educate, Enlighten, Familiarise, Foster, Groom, Guide, Improve, Indoctrinate, Inform, Instruct, Prepare, School, Teach, Train, Tutor

Coax Allure, Beckon, Beguile, Cajole, Entice, Flatter, Inveigle, Persuade, Tempt

Coddle Mollycoddle, Smother

Coerce Blackmail, Compel, Constrain, Dominate, Domineer, Enjoin

Combat Assault, Attack, Battle, Box, Embattle, Fight

Combine (PL) Unify, Unite

Comfort Aid, Allay, Alleviate, Appease, Assuage, Calm, Cheer, Console, Disburden, Ease, Embolden, Encourage,

Enhearten, Gladden, Hearten, Mollify,
Nourish, Pacify, Quieten, Reassure,
Relax, Relieve, Revive, Rock, Soothe,
Strengthen, Sustain

Command Adjure, Bid, Call, Charge, Compel,
Control, Direct, Dominate, Govern,
Instruct, Master, Order, Rule

Commend Acclaim, Applaud, Approve, Back,
Befriend, Champion, Compliment,
Honour, Praise, Promote, Recommend,
Support

Commission Appoint, Authorise, Delegate,
Empower, Enable, Engage, Enlist,
License, Ordain, Warrant

Commit (PL) Betroth, Bind, Engage, Obligate,
Pledge

Compel Blackmail, Coerce, Command,
Constrain, Drive, Enforce, Entrance, Extort,
Fascinate, Force, Impel, Instruct, Mesmerise,
Motivate, Obligate, Oblige, Press, Urge

Compensate Recompense, Restitute, Reward

Compliment Boost, Commend, Congratulate,
Exalt, Extol, Felicitate, Flatter, Greet,
Honour, Extol, Laud, Praise

Compose Align, Calm, Harmonise, Settle,
Sober, Soothe

Compromise Disturb, Embroil, Encumber,
Endanger, Ensnare, Imperil, Implicate,
Risk, Threaten, Undermine

Compute Categorise, Examine, Read, Scan,
Study

Con Beguile, Cheat, Deceive, Defraud,
Delude, Diddle, Dupe, Entrap, Fool,
Gull, Hoax, Hoodwink, Inveigle, Lure,
Swindle, Trick

Concentrate Focus, Strengthen

Concern Bother, Disquiet, Distress, Disturb,
Perturb, Trouble, Worry

Conciliate Appease, Enjoin, Mollify, Pacify,
Placate, Propitiate, Soothe

Condemn Blame, Castigate, Censure, Convict,
Criticise, Curse, Cuss, Damn, Decry,
Denounce, Outlaw, Punish, Rebuff, Reprove

Condition Accustom, Habituate, Indoctrinate,
Shape, Teach, Train

Condone Abet, Accept, Approve, Back,
Excuse, Forgive, Sanction, Support

Conduct Control, Direct, Govern, Guide,
Lead, Manage, Manoeuvre, Rule,
Shepherd

Confine Besiege, Bind, Cage, Categorise,
Constrain, Constrict, Chain, Cramp,
Encircle, Enclose, Encumber, Enslave,
Fetter, Hamper, Hold, Limit, Manacle, Pen,
Pinion, Repress, Restrain, Restrict, Shackle,
Tie, Trammel

Confirm Affirm, Approve, Authorise, Back,
Certify, Champion, Endorse, Favour,
Recommend, Validate, Verify

Confound Amaze, Astonish, Astound, Baffle,
Bamboozle, Bedevil, Befuddle, Bewilder,
Block, Confuse, Confute, Curb, Curse,
Defeat, Derange, Disturb, Dumbfound,
Elude, Embroil, Ensnare, Flabbergast, Floor,
Flummox, Foil, Frustrate, Muddle, Mystify,
Outwit, Perplex, Puzzle, Startle, Stump,
Stun, Surprise, Trouble, Unhinge, Unnerve

Confront Accost, Battle, Block, Challenge,
Dare, Defy, Disturb, Embattle, Encounter,
Face, Frustrate, Halt, Obstruct, Resist,
Tackle

Confuse Addle, Agitate, Baffle, Bamboozle,
Bedevil, Befuddle, Bemuse, Bewilder,
Cloud, Confound, Daze, Discompose,
Disconcert, Disorientate, Disturb, Dizzy,
Entangle, Faze, Flummox, Fluster,
Fuddle, Jumble, Muddle, Mystify,
Perplex, Perturb, Puzzle, Stump, Trouble,
Unhinge, Unnerve, Unsettle

Confute Confound, Crush, Expose, Negate

Congratulate   Applaud, Compliment,
   Felicitate, Praise
Congregate (PL)   Assemble, Rally
Conjoin (PL)   Rally, Unify, Unite
Conjure   Behold, Entreat, Evoke, Invoke,
   Raise, Summon
Conquer   Appropriate, Beat, Crush, Defeat,
   Demolish, Dethrone, Floor, Overcome,
   Overmaster, Overpower, Overthrow,
   Overwhelm, Prostrate, Quell, Repress,
   Rule, Subjugate, Vanquish
Consecrate   Anoint, Bless, Enshrine, Honour,
   Immortalise, Ordain, Sanctify, Treasure,
   Venerate
Conserve   Cherish, Enshrine, Immortalise,
   Retain, Treasure
Consider   Analyse, Apprehend, Contemplate,
   Evaluate, Examine, Gauge, Judge,
   Measure, Weigh
Consign   Assign, Entrust
Console   Assuage, Cheer, Comfort, Embolden,
   Encourage, Hearten, Reassure, Relieve, Soothe
Constrain, 1   Compel, Curb, Enforce
Constrain, 2   Bind, Box, Chain, Coerce, Confine,
   Constrict, Control, Cramp, Encumber, Fetter,
   Hamper, Inhibit, Necessitate, Obligate,
   Pigeonhole, Press, Pressurise, Restrain,
   Restrict, Stop, Tie, Trammel
Constrict   Chain, Choke, Confine, Constrain,
   Curb, Encumber, Fetter, Hamper,
   Restrict, Tighten, Trammel
Consume   Absorb, Chew, Devour, Engulf,
   Envelop, Overwhelm, Swallow, Swamp
Contain   Accommodate, Control, Curb,
   Enclose, Encompass, Hold, Possess,
   Subsume, Surround
Contaminate   Adulterate, Besmear, Blight,
   Damage, Debase, Defile, Dirty, Doctor,
   Foul, Impair, Infect, Poison, Pollute,
   Smear, Spoil, Stain, Taint, Vitiate

Contemplate Consider, Evaluate, Examine, Gauge, Measure, Weigh

Content Appease, Ease, Gladden, Gratify, Humour, Mollify, Placate, Please, Reconcile, Satisfy

Contest Challenge, Question

Contort Bend, Distort, Modify, Pervert, Twist, Warp

Contract Employ, Engage

Contradict Negate, Oppose, Resist

Control Check, Command, Conduct, Constrain, Contain, Curb, Direct, Dominate, Domineer, Encompass, Engineer, Govern, Manage, Manipulate, Manoeuvre, Master, Moderate, Order, Organise, Possess, Programme, Restrain, Shepherd, Subdue

Convert Adapt, Adjust, Alter, Change, Indoctrinate, Shape, Transform, Turn

Convey Bear, Transport

Convict Arrest, Condemn

Convince Assure, Persuade, Win

Cool Chill, Refresh, Sober

Copy Ape, Echo, Emulate, Imitate, Mimic, Mirror, Parrot, Reflect

Corner Box, Trap, Monopolise

Correct Amend, Chastise, Emend, Improve, Moderate, Reform, Reprimand, Reprove

Corroborate Strengthen, Support

Corrode Crumble, Dissolve, Erode

Corrupt Adulterate, Bastardise, Blemish, Bowdlerise, Bribe, Damage, Debase, Deflower, Degrade, Deprave, Demoralise, Impair, Infect, Pervert, Poison, Pollute, Taint, Violate, Vitiate

Cosset Mollycoddle, Pamper, Smother

Counsel Advise, Apprise, Caution, Edify, Educate, Enlighten, Guide, Inform, Instruct, Teach, Tutor, Warn

Counteract Balance, Neutralise

Court   Beguile, Cajole, Charm, Entice, Escort,
Inveigle, Pursue, Romance, Seduce, Woo

Cover   Circumbscribe, Encase, Encompass,
Muffle, Mute, Shield, Subsume, Veil,
Wrap

Covet   Desire, Envy

Crack, 1   Break, Burst, Fracture, Shatter,
Snap, Splinter, Split, Strike

Crack, 2   Decode

Cradle   Assuage, Cushion, Hold, Lull, Nestle,
Pet, Rock, Support

Cramp   Clog, Confine, Constrain, Encumber,
Hamper, Handicap, Hinder, Impede,
Inhibit, Limit, Oppress, Restrain,
Restrict, Trammel

Craze   Unhinge

Credit   Entrust, Honour, Thank

Cripple   Break, Damage, Debilitate, Defeat,
Demoralise, Deprive, Destroy, Disable,
Emasculate, Enervate, Frustrate, Hinder,
Impair, Immobilise, Impoverish, Injure,
Incapacitate, Maim, Mangle, Mutilate,
Paralyse, Rout, Ruin, Sabotage, Weaken

Criticise   Analyse, Appraise, Assess, Attack,
Blame, Blast, Browbeat, Castigate,
Censure, Chide, Condemn, Decry,
Denounce, Harass, Hector, Henpeck,
Knock, Nag, Pan, Scold

Cross-examine   Catechise, Challenge, Grill,
Interrogate, Interview, Investigate, Probe,
Pump, Question, Quiz

Crowd   Bump, Elbow, Henpeck, Hustle,
Nudge, Push, Shove

Crown, 1   Adorn, Decorate, Dignify, Honour,
Perfect, Reward

Crown, 2   Hit, Strike

Crucify   Execute, Persecute

Crumble   Break, Corrode, Dissolve, Disunite,
Erode, Fragment, Shatter, Splinter, Split

Crumple   Crush, Rumple

Crush Batter, Beat, Break, Bruise, Confute,
Conquer, Crumple, Defeat, Demolish,
Demoralise, Destroy, Dethrone, Dispirit,
Hammer, Humble, Humiliate, Mangle,
Mash, Oppress, Overmaster, Overpower,
Overthrow, Overwhelm, Press, Pulverise,
Quash, Repress, Rout, Ruin, Shatter,
Slaughter, Smash, Squash, Subdue,
Suppress, Tyrannise, Vanquish, Wallop

Cuddle Caress, Embrace, Encircle, Enfold,
Fondle, Hold, Hug, Pet, Squeeze

Cudgel Beat, Bludgeon, Hit, Knock

Cue Activate, Prompt, Trigger

Cuff Bang, Batter, Beat, Belt, Box, Clobber,
Hit, Knock, Smack, Sock, Strike, Whack

Cultivate Aid, Assist, Back, Better, Civilise,
Coach, Develop, Discipline, Drill,
Encourage, Edify, Educate, Elevate,
Enlighten, Enrich, Foster, Improve,
Inform, Instruct, Nurture, Perfect,
Polish, Raise Rear, Refine, School, Teach,
Train, Tutor

Cup Hold

Curb Block, Confound, Constrict, Constrain,
Contain, Control, Dampen, Delay,
Discourage, Encumber, Fetter, Gag,
Hamper, Handicap, Halt, Hinder, Hold,
Impede, Inhibit, Moderate, Muzzle,
Obstruct, Oppress, Quieten, Repress,
Restrain, Restrict, Silence, Stifle, Still,
Subdue, Suppress, Throttle, Trammel

Cure Heal, Improve, Mend, Regenerate,
Relieve, Remedy, Replenish, Restore,
Treat

Curse Abuse, Afflict, Anathematise, Bewitch,
Chide, Condemn, Confound, Cuss,
Damn, Haunt, Insult, Plague, Profane,
Threaten, Torment

Cushion, 1 Cradle, Defend, Protect, Relieve,
Shield

Cushion, 2   Deaden, Muffle, Stifle

Cuss   Blast, Condemn, Curse, Damn, Insult, Plague

Customise   Accommodate

Cut, 1   Amputate, Bite, Chop, Cleave, Dissect, Gash, Gouge, Hack, Hurt, Incise, Knife, Lacerate, Lance, Nick, Notch, Pierce, Prick, Prune, Raze, Rip, Score, Scratch, Sever, Slash, Slit, Split, Sting, Strike, Tear, Wound

Cut, 2   Disregard, Humiliate

Dab Pat, Press, Tap, Touch

Damage Abuse, Assault, Blemish, Break, Bruise, Cripple, Contaminate, Corrupt, Deface, Defame, Defile, Deprive, Harm, Hit, Hurt, Impair, Injure, Maim, Maltreat, Mar, Mistreat, Mutilate, Nick, Ruin, Sabotage, Savage, Scratch, Spoil, Taint, Weaken, Wound

D

Damn Anathematise, Blacken, Curse, Cuss, Condemn

Dampen Curb, Deaden, Depress, Discourage, Dispirit, Dissuade, Dull, Mute

Dangle Suspend

Dare Challenge, Confront, Provoke

Dash Batter, Shatter, Smash, Strike

Daze Amaze, Astonish, Astound, Baffle, Bemuse, Bewilder, Blind, Confuse, Dazzle, Distract, Dumbfound, Faze, Flabbergast, Flummox, Perplex, Puzzle, Shock, Stagger, Startle, Stun, Stupefy, Surprise

Dazzle Amaze, Astonish, Blind, Captivate, Daze, Fascinate, Flabbergast, Hypnotise, Impress, Overpower, Overwhelm, Stupefy

Deactivate Anaesthetise, Anathematise, Disable

Deaden Anaesthetise, Dampen, Diminish, Dull, Muffle, Numb, Paralyse, Quell, Quieten, Reduce, Smother, Stifle, Suppress, Tranquilise, Weaken

Debar Ban, Disallow, Exclude, Forbid, Hinder, Obstruct, Prohibit, Refuse

Debase, 1 Degrade, Disgrace, Dishonour, Humble, Humiliate, Lower, Reduce, Shame, Weaken

Debase, 2 Adulterate, Cheapen, Contaminate, Corrupt, Defile, Deprave, Downgrade, Impair, Pervert, Pollute, Taint, Vitiate

Debauch   Assault, Defile, Deflower, Demoralise,
      Deprave, Molest, Pervert, Pollute, Rape,
      Ravish, Shame, Wreck, Violate

Debilitate   Cripple, Deplete, Deprive, Devitalise,
      Diminish, Disable, Drain, Emasculate,
      Enervate, Enfeeble, Exhaust, Fatigue,
      Impoverish, Incapacitate, Invalidate,
      Paralyse, Reduce, Restrict, Sap, Tire, Under-
      mine, Unhinge, Unnerve, Weaken, Weary

Debrief   Inform

Deceive   Bamboozle, Beguile, Betray, Blind,
      Bluff, Cheat, Con, Defraud, Delude, Dupe,
      Ensnare, Entrap, Fiddle, Flatter, Fool,
      Hoax, Misguide, Mislead, Swindle, Trick

Decipher   Crack, Unravel

Deck, 1   Adorn, Beautify, Bedeck, Enrich,
      Festoon, Ornament

Deck, 2   Beat, Floor, Hit

Decline   Deny, Refuse

Deconstruct   Analyse, Dismantle

Decorate   Adorn, Bedeck, Beautify, Blazon,
      Crown, Emblazon, Enrich, Festoon,
      Ornament, Wreathe

Decoy   Allure, Bait, Ensnare, Entice, Entrap,
      Inveigle

Decriminalise   Normalise, Revert

Decry   Abuse, Belittle, Blacken, Blame, Blast,
      Censure, Condemn, Criticise, Denounce,
      Discredit, Disparage, Dispirit

Deface   Blemish, Damage, Impair, Injure, Mar

Defame   Abuse, Accuse, Blame, Damage,
      Denigrate, Denounce, Discredit,
      Disgrace, Dishonour, Disparage, Dispirit,
      Dispraise, Knock, Malign, Shame,
      Slander, Tarnish, Vilify

Defeat   Beat, Break, Confound, Conquer,
      Cripple, Crush, Dethrone, Finish, Floor,
      Foil, Nullify, Outdo, Overpower, Overthrow,
      Overwhelm, Quash, Quell, Rebuff, Thrash,
      Thwart, Trounce, Vanquish

Defend   Arm, Champion, Cushion, Escort,
Guard, Patronise, Protect, Safeguard,
Secure, Shelter, Shield, Support

Defile   Besmear, Blacken, Contaminate,
Damage, Debase, Debauch, Deflower,
Desecrate, Dirty, Foul, Impair, Pollute,
Shame, Smear, Soil, Stain, Taint, Violate

D

Deflate   Devalue, Disappoint, Disconcert,
Dispirit, Humble, Humiliate, Milk,
Puncture

Deflect   Avert, Avoid, Dissuade, Intercept,
Misdirect, Obstruct, Rebuff, Redirect,
Repel, Stop

Deflower   Corrupt, Debauch, Defile, Molest,
Rape, Ravish

Deform   Distort, Impair, Mutilate, Pervert,
Ruin, Spoil, Twist, Warp

Defraud   Bamboozle, Beguile, Bluff, Cheat,
Con, Deceive, Delude, Diddle, Dupe,
Fleece, Fool, Hoax, Rob, Swindle, Trick

Defrost   Melt

Defy   Beat, Better, Challenge, Confront,
Crush, Disobey, Provoke, Reject, Scorn,
Thwart

Degrade   Affront, Cheapen, Corrupt, Debase,
Demean, Demote, Deprave, Discredit,
Downgrade, Humble, Humiliate, Insult,
Patronise, Pervert, Reduce, Shame

Dehumanise   Pervert

Deify   Admire, Adore, Adulate, Beatify, Exalt,
Idolise, Immortalise, Revere, Sanctify,
Venerate, Worship

Deject   Delay, Demoralise, Discourage,
Dishearten

Delay   Block, Curb, Deject, Detain,
Encumber, Hinder, Impede, Postpone,
Restrain, Thwart

Delegate   Appoint, Assign, Authorise,
Commission, Empower, Enable, Entitle,
Sanction, Warrant

Delight Allure, Amuse, Attract, Beguile, Bewitch, Captivate, Charm, Cheer, Enamour, Enchant, Engage, Enrapture, Entertain, Enthrall, Entrance, Excite, Exhilarate, Fascinate, Gladden, Gratify, Please, Pleasure, Seduce, Spellbind, Thrill

Deliver Acquit, Discharge, Disencumber, Disenthrall, Emancipate, Free, Liberate, Redeem, Release, Rescue, Unchain, Unfetter, Unshackle

Delude Bamboozle, Bluff, Cheat, Con, Deceive, Defraud, Dupe, Fool, Gull, Hoax, Hoodwink, Kid, Misguide, Mislead, Outwit, Swindle, Trick

Deluge Bury, Drown, Engulf, Envelop, Overwhelm, Swamp

Demarcate Downgrade, Limit

Demean Belittle, Cheapen, Degrade, Devalue, Humble, Humiliate

Demobilise Liberate, Normalise, Regularise

Demolish Annihilate, Batter, Beat, Blast, Break, Bulldoze, Conquer, Crush, Destroy, Devastate, Dismantle, Flatten, Floor, Knock, Obliterate, Overthrow, Overturn, Plunder, Pulverise, Quash, Quell, Ravage, Raze, Rout, Ruin, Shatter, Smash, Suppress, Vanquish

Demoralise Break, Corrupt, Cripple, Crush, Debauch, Deject, Deprave, Depress, Devitalise, Discourage, Dishearten, Dismay, Dispirit, Enervate, Impair, Sap, Undermine, Weaken

Demote Degrade, Depose, Devalue, Downgrade, Humble, Punish, Reduce, Shame

Denigrate Berate, Blacken, Cheapen, Defame, Discredit, Insult, Revile

Denounce Anathematise, Accuse, Arraign, Attack, Berate, Castigate, Censure, Condemn, Criticise, Decry, Defame, Disparage, Dispraise, Impeach, Indict, Revile, Vilify

Deny Decline, Refuse

Deplete Debilitate, Deprive, Devitalise,
Diminish, Drain, Empty, Enfeeble,
Exhaust, Fatigue, Impair, Impoverish,
Reduce, Sap, Undermine, Weaken

Deploy Activate, Employ, Use, Utilise

Depose Demote, Dethrone, Disbar, Oust,
Overthrow, Sack,, Suspend, Topple

Deprave Abuse, Corrupt, Debase, Debauch,
Degrade, Demoralise, Pervert

Deprecate Abuse

Depress Chill, Dampen, Demoralise,
Desolate, Discourage, Dishearten,
Dispirit, Oppress, Sadden, Sober, Weaken

Deprive Cripple, Damage, Debilitate, Deplete,
Devitalise, Dilute, Enfeeble, Expropriate,
Fatigue, Impair, Impoverish, Incapacitate,
Lessen, Reduce, Rob, Sap, Weaken

Derail Destabilise

Derange Agitate, Confound, Destabilise,
Deviate, Disconcert, Dizzy, Impair,
Muddle, Perturb, Pervert, Puzzle,
Trouble, Twist, Unhinge, Unsteady, Upset

Deride Mock, Ridicule, Scorn

Desecrate Defile, Violate, Pervert, Profane

Desert Abandon, Betray, Forsake, Jilt, Leave,
Maroon, Neglect, Reject, Relinquish,
Shun, Spurn

Designate Appoint, Choose, Elect, Nominate,
Pick, Select

Desolate Depress

Despoil Destroy, Devastate, Harry, Pillage,
Ransack, Rape, Ravage, Rob, Steal

Despise Revile, Scorn

Destabilise Derail, Derange, Unhinge, Unsteady

Destroy Abolish, Annihilate, Batter, Blast,
Bludgeon, Break, Cancel, Cripple, Crush,
Demolish, Despoil, Devastate, Efface,
Eliminate, Eradicate, Excise, Execute,
Expunge,, Exterminate, Extirpate,
Finish, Incinerate, Kill, Mangle, Murder,

Nullify, Obliterate, Plunder, Quash,
Quell, Ravage, Raze, Rout, Ruin, Shatter,
Slaughter, Smash, Trash, Vandalise,
Vanquish, Wreck, Zap

Detach (PL)   Isolate, Separate, Wrest

Detain   Delay, Hinder, Hold, Imprison,
Inhibit, Restrict, Retain, Stop

Detect   Catch, Discover, Expose, Unmask

Deter   Block, Discourage, Dispirit, Dissuade,
Frighten, Hamper, Hinder, Impede,
Intimidate, Obstruct, Prohibit

Dethrone   Conquer, Crush, Defeat, Depose,
Dispossess, Overthrow, Topple

Devalue   Adulterate, Cheapen, Deflate,
Demean, Demote, Discredit, Downgrade,
Reduce, Shame, Subordinate, Weaken

Devastate   Demolish, Despoil, Destroy,
Plunder, Ravage, Raze, Rout, Ruin, Sack,
Shatter, Smash, Wreck

Develop   Civilise, Coach, Cultivate,
Discipline, Drill, Edify, Educate,
Enlighten, Foster, Improve, Instruct,
Rear, Refine, School, Teach, Train, Tutor

Deviate   Derange, Pervert, Twist, Warp

Devitalise   Debilitate, Demoralise, Deplete,
Deprive, Disable, Diminish, Drain,
Enervate, Enfeeble, Exhaust, Fatigue,
Incapacitate, Jade, Paralyse, Sap, Tire,
Undermine, Unhinge, Weaken

Devour   Appropriate, Consume, Gobble, Guzzle

Diddle   Cheat, Con, Defraud, Fleece, Fool,
Hoax, Hoodwink, Swindle

Dig   Jab, Prod

Digest   Absorb, Process

Dignify   Aggrandise, Better, Crown, Elevate,
Ennoble, Exalt, Glorify, Grace, Honour,
Knight, Revere, Sanctify, Venerate

Dilute   Adulterate, Deprive, Sap, Weaken

Dim   Cloud, Eclipse, Efface, Excise, Obscure,
Shroud

Diminish   Deaden, Debilitate, Deplete, Devitalise, Drain, Enfeeble, Exhaust, Fatigue, Impoverish, Lessen, Lower, Reduce, Sap, Undercut, Undermine, Weaken

Direct   Command, Compel, Control, Conduct, Dominate, Focus, Govern, Guide, Lead, Manage, Manoeuvre, Motivate, Navigate, Orientate, Rule, School, Steer, Teach, Tutor

Dirty   Adulterate, Besmear, Contaminate, Defile, Foul, Pollute, Smear, Soil, Stain, Taint

Disable   Break, Cripple, Deactivate, Debilitate, Devitalise, Disarm, Enervate, Enfeeble, Exhaust, Hinder, Hurt, Immobilise, Impair, Incapacitate, Invalidate, Maim, Paralyse, Reduce, Restrict, Sabotage, Sap, Undercut, Undermine, Unhinge, Weaken, Wing, Wound

Disaffect   Disappoint, Disillusion, Embitter, Envenom, Poison, Sour

Disallow   Ban, Bar, Debar, Exclude, Forbid, Prohibit

Disappoint   Deflate, Discourage, Disconcert, Disillusion, Dispirit, Dissatisfy, Frustrate, Jade

Disarm   Disable, Dissolve, Melt, Thaw, Unnerve, Weaken, Win

Disbar   Depose, Eject, Exclude

Disbelieve   Mistrust

Disburden   Allay, Alleviate, Appease, Assuage, Calm, Comfort, Ease, Lighten, Mollify, Pacify, Quieten, Relax, Relieve, Soothe, Still, Tranquillise

Discard   Abandon, Abjure, Betray, Discharge, Disclaim, Dislodge, Dismiss, Drop, Evacuate, Expel, Forsake, Leave, Oust, Reject, Relinquish, Renounce, Sack, Spurn

Discharge   Absolve, Acquit, Clear, Deliver, Disencumber, Disengage, Disentangle,

Disenthrall, Discard, Dismiss, Eject,
Emancipate, Enfranchise, Evacuate,
Exonerate, Expel, Fire, Free, Liberate,
Oust, Pardon, Redeem, Release, Sack,
Unburden, Unshackle, Untie

Discipline   Chasten, Chastise, Civilise, Coach,
Cultivate, Develop, Drill, Edify, Educate,
Enlighten, Foster, Govern, Indoctrinate,
Inform, Instruct, Mould, Punish, School,
Subjugate, Tame, Teach, Train, Tutor

Disclaim   Discard, Disown, Rebuke, Reject,
Renounce, Spurn

Discomfit   Appall, Confuse, Discomfort,
Discompose, Disconcert, Distress,
Disturb, Embarrass, Floor, Fluster,
Perturb, Ruffle, Shame, Upset

Discomfort   Embarrass, Floor, Perturb, Ruffle,
Trouble, Upset

Discompose   Confuse, Disconcert, Displease,
Dissatisfy, Distress, Embarrass, Fluster,
Perturb, Shame

Disconcert   Agitate, Baffle, Confuse, Deflate,
Derange, Disappoint, Distract, Distress,
Discompose, Floor, Fluster, Frighten,
Perturb, Rattle, Trouble, Unnerve,
Unsettle, Upset

Disconnect (PL)   Isolate

Discourage   Caution, Chill, Curb, Dampen,
Deject, Demoralise, Depress, Deter,
Disappoint, Dishearten, Dismay, Dispirit,
Dissuade, Hinder, Impede, Inhibit,
Obstruct, Oppose, Oppress, Prohibit,
Rebuff, Repress, Suppress

Discover   Detect, Unearth

Discredit   Belittle, Cheapen, Decry, Defame,
Degrade, Denigrate, Devalue, Disgrace,
Slander, Vilify, Wrong

Dissect   Analyse, Examine, Inspect, Probe,
Scrutinise, Study, Vet

Disempower   Castrate, Emasculate

Disenchant   Disillusion, Sour

Disencumber   Acquit, Alleviate, Deliver,
          Discharge, Disengage, Disentangle,
          Disenthrall, Emancipate, Enfranchise,
          Free, Liberate, Rescue, Release, Relieve,
          Unburden, Unchain, Unfetter, Unleash,
          Unshackle, Untie

Disengage   Clear, Discharge, Disencumber,
          Disentangle, Disenthrall, Emancipate,
          Free, Liberate, Release, Unburden,
          Unchain, Undo, Unfetter, Unhook,
          Unshackle, Untie

Disentangle   Clear, Discharge, Disencumber,
          Disengage, Disenthrall, Emancipate, Free,
          Liberate, Redeem, Release, Relieve,
          Unburden, Unchain, Undo, Unfetter, Un-
          hook. Unleash, Unravel, Unshackle, Untie

Disenthrall   Deliver, Discharge, Disencumber,
          Disengage, Disentangle, Emancipate,
          Enfranchise, Free, Liberate, Rescue,
          Release, Unburden, Unchain, Unfetter,
          Unleash, Unshackle, Untie

Disgrace   Debase, Defame, Discredit, Humble,
          Humiliate, Shame, Taint

Disgust   Appall, Horrify, Nauseate, Offend,
          Outrage, Repel, Repulse, Scandalise,
          Shock, Sicken

Dishearten   Chill, Deject, Demoralise, Depress,
          Discourage, Dismay, Dispirit, Enervate,
          Intimidate, Oppress, Repress, Sadden

Dishonour   Blacken, Debase, Defame,
          Disparage, Pollute, Shame, Taint, Wrong

Disillusion   Alienate, Disaffect, Disenchant,
          Embitter, Sour

Dislodge   Discard, Dismiss, Dispossess, Eject,
          Evacuate, Expel, Fire, Oust, Remove, Sack

Dismantle   Deconstruct, Demolish

Dismay   Appall, Demoralise, Discourage,
          Dishearten, Dispirit, Enervate, Sadden

Dismember   Mutilate

D

Dismiss   Abolish, Banish, Discard, Discharge,
         Dislodge, Eject, Exile, Expel, Fire, Oust,
         Remove, Sack

Disobey   Defy, Disregard, Ignore

Disorientate   Befuddle, Cloud, Confuse

Disown   Disclaim, Reject, Repudiate, Shun

Disparage   Abuse, Accuse, Blame, Charge,
         Cheapen, Decry, Defame, Denounce,
         Dishonour, Impeach, Reproach, Slander,
         Vilify

Dispirit   Break, Cheapen, Crush, Dampen, Decry,
         Defame, Deflate, Demoralise, Depress, Deter,
         Disappoint, Discourage, Dishearten, Dismay,
         Enervate, Intimidate, Oppress, Sadden

Displace   Banish, Exile, Override

Displease   Aggrieve, Annoy, Discompose,
         Dissatisfy, Disturb, Irk, Offend, Perturb

Dispossess   Banish, Dethrone, Dislodge, Eject,
         Evacuate, Exile, Expel, Expropriate, Fire,
         Oust, Sack

Dispraise   Attack, Belittle, Defame,
         Denounce, Pan

Disqualify   Ban, Exclude, Prohibit

Disquiet   Agitate, Concern, Dizzy, Perturb

Disregard   Avoid, Cut, Disobey, Drop,
         Eliminate, Exclude, Ignore, Neglect,
         Overlook, Reject, Repudiate, Spurn

Disrupt   Disturb, Hamper, Heckle, Impede,
         Interrupt, Sabotage, Upset

Dissatisfy   Disappoint, Discompose,
         Displease, Disturb, Upset

Dissect   Analyse, Scrutinise, Study, Vet

Disseminate   Destroy

Dissolve   Corrode, Crumble, Disarm, Erode, Melt

Dissuade   Advise, Caution, Dampen, Deflect,
         Deter, Discourage, Warn

Distance   Alienate

Distend   Aggrandise, Boost, Expand, Inflate, Swell

Distinguish   Adorn, Elevate, Glorify, Grace,
         Honour

Distort   Bend, Contort, Deform, Mangle,
   Pervert, Warp
Distract   Addle, Bemuse, Blind, Bother,
   Daze, Disconcert, Divert, Muddle,
   Puzzle, Throw, Upset, Worry
Distress   Afflict, Agitate, Alarm, Annoy,
   Bedevil, Bother, Concern, Discompose,
   Disconcert, Disturb, Fluster, Fret,
   Mortify, Sadden, Trouble, Unnerve,
   Upset, Vex, Worry
Disturb   Addle, Affect, Agitate, Alarm, Annoy,
   Badger, Bother, Compromise, Concern,
   Confound, Confront, Confuse, Displease,
   Disrupt, Dissatisfy, Distress, Dizzy,
   Embroil, Faze, Fluster, Fret, Harass,
   Harry, Haunt, Muddle, Perplex, Perturb,
   Pester, Plague, Rattle, Rock, Ruffle,
   Shock, Stir, Trouble, Unsettle, Upset,
   Vex, Wobble, Worry
Disunite (PL)   Break, Crumble, Divide,
   Fragment, Shatter, Splinter, Split, Untie
Ditch   Abandon, Drop, Forsake, Jilt, Reject
Divert, 1   Avert, Distract, Intercept, Obstruct,
   Redirect, Stall
Divert, 2   Engage, Entertain, Interest, Regale
Divide (PL)   Bisect, Cleave, Disunite,
   Separate, Split, Sunder
Divorce   Forsake, Reject
Dizzy   Addle, Agitate, Confuse, Derange,
   Disturb, Disquiet, Fluster, Ruffle, Unsettle
Doctor, 1   Advise
Doctor, 2   Adulterate, Contaminate
Dodge   Avoid, Elude, Escape, Evade, Flee,
   Outrun, Shirk, Shun, Sidestep
Dominate   Coerce, Command, Control,
   Direct, Govern, Master, Monopolise,
   Overmaster, Overpower, Repress, Rule,
   Steer, Tyrannise
Domineer   Coerce, Control, Govern,
   Overmaster, Overpower, Rule, Tyrannise

D

Douse   Drench, Plunge, Soak

Downgrade   Debase, Degrade, Demarcate, Demote, Devalue, Humble, Lower

Drain   Debilitate, Deplete, Devitalise, Diminish, Empty, Enervate, Enfeeble, Exhaust, Fatigue, Impoverish, Incapacitate, Jade, Milk, Reduce, Sap, Tire, Weary

Draw   Beckon, Engage, Extract, Pull, Tug, Yank

Drench   Douse, Imbue, Infuse, Saturate, Soak

Dress   Attire, Clothe, Groom

Drill, 1   Coach, Cultivate, Develop, Discipline, Edify, Educate, Enlighten, Exercise, Groom, Indoctrinate, Inform, Instruct, School, Teach, Train, Tutor

Drill, 2   Pierce

Drive   Compel, Encourage, Force, Goad, Impel, Motivate, Propel, Push, Spur, Stimulate, Thrust, Urge

Drop   Abandon, Discard, Disregard, Ditch, Dump, Eject, Eliminate, Exclude, Expel, Forsake, Jilt, Leave, Reject, Spurn

Drown   Bury, Deluge, Empty, Engulf, Envelop, Plunge, Sink, Submerge

Dull   Anaesthetise, Dampen, Deaden, Numb, Quieten

Dumbfound   Amaze, Astonish, Astound, Baffle, Befuddle, Confound, Daze, Flabbergast, Floor, Perplex, Puzzle, Stagger, Stump, Stun

Dump   Abandon, Drop, Forsake, Reject

Dupe   Bamboozle, Beguile, Cheat, Con, Deceive, Defraud, Delude, Fool, Gull, Hoax, Hoodwink, Outwit, Swindle, Trick, Victimise

Ease Aid, Allay, Alleviate, Appease, Assuage,
    Calm, Comfort, Content, Disburden,
    Lighten, Mollify, Pacify, Quieten,
    Relax, Relieve, Sedate, Settle,
    Smooth, Soothe, Tranquillise

Echo Ape, Copy, Mirror, Parrot, Reflect

Eclipse, 1 Dim, Extinguish, Obscure,
    Shroud, Veil

Eclipse, 2 Exceed, Excel, Outdo, Outshine,
    Overshadow, Surpass, Transcend

Edify Apprise, Civilise, Coach, Counsel,
    Cultivate, Develop, Discipline, Drill, Educate,
    Elevate, Enlighten, Exercise, Foster, Guide,
    Improve, Indoctrinate, Inform, Instruct,
    Nurture, School, Teach, Train, Tutor

Educate Advise, Apprise, Civilise, Coach,
    Counsel, Cultivate, Develop, Discipline,
    Drill, Edify, Elevate, Enlighten, Enrich,
    Foster, Groom, Guide, Improve, Indoc-
    trinate, Inform, Instruct, Mould, Nurture,
    Refine, School, Shape, Teach, Tutor, Train

Efface, 1 Cancel, Destroy, Eradicate, Excise,
    Expunge, Extirpate, Obliterate, Raze

Efface, 2 Dim, Humble, Lower

Eject Banish, Boot, Disbar, Discharge,
    Dislodge, Dismiss, Dispossess, Drop,
    Eliminate, Exclude, Exile, Expel,
    Extrude, Fire, Oust, Reject, Remove,
    Sack, Spurn

Elate Animate, Boost, Brighten, Cheer,
    Elevate, Excite, Exhilarate, Gladden,
    Hearten, Raise, Rouse, Uplift

Elbow Bump, Crowd, Hustle, Jab, Jostle,
    Knock, Nudge, Prod, Push, Shove

Elect Appoint, Choose, Designate, Endorse,
    Pick, Select

E

Electrify Activate, Amaze, Animate, Astonish, Energise, Enliven, Excite, Fire, Galvanise, Inspirit, Invigorate, Jolt, Motivate, Quicken, Rouse, Shock, Startle, Stimulate, Stir, Thrill, Vitalise

Elevate, 1 Cultivate, Edify, Educate, Empower, Enlighten, Grace, Heighten, Improve, Inform, Instruct, Nurture, Refine, School, Teach

Elevate, 2 Augment, Aggrandise, Dignify, Distinguish, Ennoble, Exalt, Glorify, Honour, Promote, Raise, Strengthen, Swell, Upgrade, Uplift

Elevate, 3 Animate, Boost, Brighten, Cheer, Elate, Exalt, Excite, Exhilarate, Hearten, Hoist, Lift, Rouse

Eliminate, 1 Banish, Disregard, Drop, Eject, Exclude, Expel, Reject

Eliminate, 2 Annihilate, Destroy, Eradicate, Exterminate, Kill, Murder, Slay, Terminate

Elude, 1 Avoid, Dodge, Escape, Evade, Flee, Foil, Forestall, Hedge, Outrun, Outwit, Shirk, Shun, Sidestep

Elude, 2 Baffle, Block, Confound, Frustrate, Puzzle, Stump, Thwart

Emancipate Deliver, Discharge, Disencumber, Disengage, Disentangle, Disenthrall, Enfranchise, Free, Liberate, Release, Rescue, Unchain, Unfetter, Unleash, Unshackle, Untie

Emasculate Castrate, Cripple, Debilitate, Disempower, Enervate, Impoverish, Unman, Weaken

Embarrass Discomfort, Discompose, Fluster, Humiliate, Shame

Embattle Challenge, Combat, Confront

Embed Plant, Root

Embitter Aggravate, Alienate, Disaffect, Disillusion, Envenom, Poison, Sour

Emblazon, 1 Adorn, Decorate, Ornament

Emblazon, 2   Extol, Glorify, Laud, Praise,
Proclaim, Trumpet

Embolden   Animate, Assure, Cheer, Comfort,
Console, Encourage, Fire, Fortify,
Hearten, Incite, Inflame, Inspire, Inspirit,
Invigorate, Nerve, Rally, Reassure,
Rouse, Stiffen, Stimulate, Stir,
Strengthen, Sustain, Vitalise

Embrace, 1   Caress, Clasp, Clinch, Clutch,
Cuddle, Encircle, Enclasp, Enclose,
Encompass, Enfold, Envelop, Enwrap,
Grab, Grasp, Hold, Hug, Nuzzle, Press,
Seize, Squeeze, Swathe, Wrap

Embrace, 2   Accept, Admit, Adopt, Enjoin,
Espouse, Incorporate, Welcome

Embroil   Compromise, Confound, Disturb,
Enmesh, Ensnare, Entangle, Implicate,
Involve, Muddle, Snare

Emend   Adapt, Amend, Censor, Correct,
Improve, Polish

Employ   Appoint, Contract, Deploy, Engage,
Enlist, Occupy, Recruit, Retain, Use, Utilise

Empower   Arm, Authorise, Capacitate,
Commission, Delegate, Elevate, Enable,
Entitle, License, Permit, Sanction

Empty   Deplete, Drain, Drown, Exhaust

Emulate   Copy, Follow, Imitate, Mimic

Enable   Authorise, Commission, Delegate,
Entitle, Facilitate, License, Permit,
Qualify, Sanction

Enamour   Allure, Arrest, Attract, Beguile,
Bewitch, Captivate, Charm, Delight,
Enchant, Endear, Engage, Enrapture,
Enthral, Entrance, Fascinate, Mesmerise,
Spellbind, Win

Enchant   Allure, Arrest, Attract, Beguile,
Bewitch, Captivate, Catch, Charm, Delight,
Enamour, Endear, Engage, Enrapture,
Enthral, Entrance, Fascinate, Hold,
Mesmerise, Mystify, Ravish, Spellbind, Win

E

Encircle   Besiege, Circle, Circumscribe,
Confine, Cuddle, Embrace, Enclose,
Encompass, Enfold, Entrap, Envelop,
Enwrap, Grasp, Hug, Surround, Wreathe

Enclasp   Embrace

Enclose   Circle, Circumscribe, Confine,
Contain, Embrace, Encircle, Enwrap,
Enfold, Envelope, Hold, Hug, Pen,
Shroud, Surround, Swathe, Wrap

Encompass   Besiege, Circle, Circumscribe,
Contain, Control, Cover, Embrace,
Encircle, Enclose, Enfold, Engulf,
Envelop, Enwrap, Embrace, Hold, Hug,
Include, Incorporate, Involve, Subsume,
Surround, Swathe, Wrap

Encounter   Confront, Engage, Face, Fight

Encourage   Abet, Advise, Advocate, Aid,
Animate, Applaud, Arouse, Assist,
Assure, Augment, Back, Befriend, Bolster,
Boost, Champion, Cheer, Comfort,
Console, Cultivate, Drive, Embolden,
Enhearten, Enthuse, Favour, Feed, Fire,
Fortify, Forward, Foster, Fuel, Further,
Galvanise, Goad, Hearten, Help, Incite,
Inflame, Influence, Inspire, Inspirit,
Invigorate, Lift, Motivate, Nerve,
Nourish, Nurse, Nurture, Patronise,
Persuade, Prod, Promote, Rally, Reassure,
Revive, Rouse, Spur, Stimulate, Stir,
Stoke, Strengthen, Succour, Support,
Sustain, Uphold, Urge, Vitalise, Will

Encumber   Bind, Burden, Chain, Clog,
Compromise, Confine, Constrain,
Constrict, Contain, Cramp, Curb, Delay,
Enmesh, Enslave, Ensnare, Entangle,
Fetter, Hamper, Handicap, Hinder,
Impede, Implicate, Inconvenience,
Involve, Manacle, Obstruct, Oppress,
Overload, Restrain, Restrict, Retard,
Saddle, Shackle, Tie, Trammel

Endanger   Ambush, Compromise, Imperil,
   Implicate, Terrorise, Threaten
Endear   Attract, Bind, Captivate, Charm,
   Enamour, Enchant, Engage, Enrapture,
   Enthrall, Entrance
Endorse   Abet, Advocate, Affirm, Approve,
   Authorise, Back, Confirm, Elect, Entitle,
   Favour, Permit, Ratify, Recommend,
   Sanction, Support, Sustain, Vindicate,
   Warrant
Endow   Award, Enrich, Favour, Furnish
Endure   Abide, Bear, Suffer, Support, Tolerate,
   Weather, Withstand
Energise   Activate, Animate, Arouse, Electrify,
   Engage, Enliven, Generate, Goad,
   Hearten, Inspirit, Instigate, Invigorate,
   Motivate, Quicken, Refresh, Regenerate,
   Rouse, Stimulate, Stir, Spur, Vitalise
Enervate   Break, Cripple, Debilitate,
   Demoralise, Devitalise, Disable,
   Dishearten, Dismay, Dispirit, Drain,
   Emasculate, Enfeeble, Exhaust, Fatigue,
   Impoverish, Incapacitate, Jade, Paralyse,
   Reduce, Restrict, Sap, Tire, Weaken
Enfeeble   Break, Debilitate, Deplete, Deprive,
   Devitalise, Disable, Diminish, Drain,
   Enervate, Exhaust, Fatigue, Incapacitate,
   Jade, Paralyse, Restrict, Sap, Tire, Undercut,
   Undermine, Unhinge, Unnerve, Weaken
Enfold   Circle, Circumscribe, Clasp, Cuddle,
   Embrace, Encircle, Enclose, Encompass,
   Engulf, Envelop, Enwrap, Hold, Hug,
   Shroud, Surround, Swathe, Wrap,
   Wreathe
Enforce   Compel, Constrain, Obligate,
   Pressurise, Prosecute, Urge
Enfranchise   Capacitate, Discharge,
   Disencumber, Disenthrall, Emancipate,
   Free, Liberate, Release, Unchain,
   Unfetter, Unshackle

E

Engage, 1   Attract, Allure, Arrest, Beguile,
Betroth, Captivate, Charm, Delight,
Divert, Draw, Enamour, Enchant,
Encounter, Endear, Energise, Engross,
Enrapture, Enthral, Entrance, Fascinate,
Grip, Hold, Hook, Hypnotise, Interest,
Involve, Mesmerise

Engage, 2   Appoint, Bind, Commission,
Commit, Contract, Employ, Enlist,
Enrol, Obligate, Occupy, Recruit, Retain,
Utilise

Engineer   Control, Manipulate, Manouevre,
Work

Engross   Arrest, Captivate, Engage, Engulf,
Entrance, Envelop, Fascinate, Fixate,
Grip, Hold, Interest, Involve,
Monopolise, Occupy, Rivet, Spellbind

Engulf   Arrest, Consume, Deluge, Drown,
Encompass, Enfold, Engross, Envelop,
Hold, Involve, Overwhelm, Preoccupy,
Swamp

Enhearten   Boost, Cheer, Comfort,
Encourage, Enthuse, Fire, Galvanise,
Generate, Hearten, Inspire, Inspirit

Enjoin   Coerce, Conciliate, Embrace, Include,
Incorporate

Enkindle   Arouse, Awaken, Excite, Fire,
Generate, Ignite, Incite, Inflame, Inspire,
Invigorate, Kindle, Provoke

Enlarge   Augment

Enlighten   Acquaint, Advise, Apprise, Civilise,
Coach, Counsel, Cultivate, Develop,
Discipline, Drill, Edify, Educate, Elevate,
Foster, Guide, Improve, Inform, Instruct,
Nurture, School, Teach, Train, Tutor

Enlist   Appoint, Commission, Employ,
Engage, Obtain, Procure, Recruit, Retain

Enliven   Activate, Amuse, Animate, Arouse,
Awaken, Brighten, Cheer, Electrify,
Energise, Excite, Exhilarate, Fire,

Freshen, Generate, Gladden, Hearten,
Inspire, Inspirit, Invigorate, Light,
Motivate, Quicken, Refresh, Restore,
Revive, Rouse, Stimulate, Titivate,
Vitalise, Waken

Enmesh   Catch, Embroil, Encumber, Ensnare,
Entangle, Entrap, Implicate, Involve,
Snare, Trammel, Trap

Ennoble   Aggrandise, Dignify, Elevate,
Entitle, Exalt, Glorify, Honour

Enrage   Aggravate, Impassion, Incense,
Incite, Inflame, Infuriate, Madden,
Outrage, Provoke

Enrapture   Beguile, Bewitch, Captivate,
Charm, Delight, Enamour, Enchant,
Endear, Engage, Entertain, Enthral,
Entrance, Fascinate, Hypnotise,
Mesmerise, Ravish, Spellbind, Thrill

Enrich, 1   Adorn, Award, Beautify, Bedeck,
Deck, Decorate, Favour, Festoon,
Furnish, Ornament, Reward

Enrich, 2   Cultivate, Educate, Endow

Enrol   Appoint, Engage

Enshrine   Adore, Adulate, Cherish,
Consecrate, Conserve, Honour, Idolise,
Immortalise, Prize, Treasure, Value,
Venerate, Worship

Enslave   Bind, Chain, Confine, Encumber,
Fetter, Hold, Manacle, Pinion, Shackle

Ensnare   Ambush, Capture, Catch, Confound,
Deceive, Decoy, Encumber, Enmesh,
Entangle, Embroil, Hijack, Hook,
Implicate, Induce, Involve, Lure, Nab,
Net, Seduce, Snare, Trammel, Trap

Entangle   Catch, Confuse, Embroil,
Encumber, Enmesh, Ensnare, Implicate,
Involve, Muddle, Net, Snare, Trammel,
Trap

Entertain   Amuse, Delight, Divert, Enrapture,
Host, Intrigue, Regale

E

Enthral   Beguile, Bewitch, Captivate, Charm,
    Delight, Enamour, Enchant, Endear, Engage,
    Enrapture, Entrance, Fascinate, Hypnotise,
    Intrigue, Mesmerise, Rivet, Spellbind
Enthuse   Encourage, Enhearten, Excite, Rally
Entice   Allure, Attract, Beckon, Beguile,
    Cajole, Coax, Court, Decoy, Entrap,
    Fascinate, Induce, Inveigle, Lure,
    Persuade, Persue, Seduce, Tempt, Woo
Entitle   Authorise, Delegate, Empower,
    Enable, Endorse, Ennoble, License,
    Permit, Qualify, Sanction, Warrant
Entrance   Beguile, Bewitch, Captivate,
    Charm, Compel, Delight, Enamour,
    Enchant, Endear, Engross, Enthral,
    Enrapture, Fascinate, Hold, Hypnotise,
    Involve, Mesmerise, Ravish, Spellbind
Entrap   Abduct, Bait, Bamboozle, Con, Deceive,
    Decoy, Entice, Hoax, Hook, Induce,
    Inveigle, Lure, Net, Seduce, Snare, Trick
Entreat   Beg, Beseech, Conjure, Implore,
    Importune, Petition, Solicit, Urge
Entrust   Consign, Credit
Entwine (PL)   Join, Link, Tie
Envelop   Absorb, Circle, Circumbscribe,
    Clasp, Consume, Deluge, Drown,
    Embrace, Encircle, Enclose, Encompass,
    Enfold, Engulf, Engross, Enwrap, Hold,
    Hug, Overwhelm, Shroud, Surround,
    Swamp, Swathe, Wrap
Envenom   Alienate, Disaffect, Embitter,
    Poison, Sour
Enwrap   Clasp, Embrace, Encircle, Enclose,
    Encompass, Enfold, Envelop, Hold,
    Shroud, Swathe, Wrap
Equal   Match
Equalise   Balance
Equip   Accommodate, Arm, Furnish, Prepare
Eradicate   Abolish, Annihilate, Banish, Cancel,
    Destroy, Efface, Eliminate, Excise, Expunge,

Exterminate, Extinguish, Extirpate, Kill, Obliterate, Raze

Erode   Crumble, Dissolve

Escape   Avoid, Dodge, Elude, Evade, Flee, Frustrate, Outrun, Shirk, Shun

Escort   Accompany, Attend, Chaperone, Court, Defend, Guard, Guide, Lead, Safeguard

Espouse   Accept, Adopt, Back, Embrace, Marry, Support, Wed, Welcome

Esteem   Admire, Respect, Revere, Value

Estimate   Analyse, Appraise, Assess, Calculate, Examine, Gauge, Measure, Value

Evacuate   Discard, Discharge, Dislodge, Dispossess, Eject, Exile, Expel, Oust, Remove

Evade   Avoid, Dodge, Elude, Escape, Flee, Outrun, Parry, Shirk, Shun, Sidestep, Stall

Evaluate   Analyse, Appraise, Assess, Consider, Contemplate, Estimate, Gauge, Measure, Weigh

Evoke   Beckon, Call, Conjure, Rouse, Summon

Exacerbate   Aggravate

Exalt   Acclaim, Adore, Adulate, Aggrandise, Beatify, Boost, Compliment, Deify, Dignify, Elevate, Ennoble, Glorify, Hail, Hearten, Heighten, Honour, Idolise, Lift, Praise, Promote, Raise, Salute, Strengthen, Swell

Examine   Analyse, Compute, Consider, Contemplate, Disect, Estimate, Gauge, Peruse, Read, Scan, Scrutinise, Study, Test, Weigh

Exasperate   Aggravate, Annoy, Antagonise, Incense, Infuriate, Irritate, Provoke, Weary

Exceed   Better, Eclipse, Excel, Outdo, Outshine, Surpass, Transcend

Excel   Eclipse, Exceed

Excise   Annihilate, Cancel, Destroy, Dim, Efface, Eradicate, Extirpate, Obliterate, Remove

Excite   Animate, Arouse, Astonish, Awaken,
     Boost, Brighten, Captivate, Cheer, Delight,
     Elate, Electrify, Elevate, Enkindle, Enliven,
     Enthuse, Exhilarate, Fan, Fire, Fluster,
     Galvanise, Hearten, Impassion, Incite,
     Infect, Inflame, Inspire, Inspirit, Intoxicate,
     Invigorate, Jolt, Kindle, Motivate, Quicken,
     Provoke, Rouse, Shock, Spark, Startle,
     Stimulate, Stoke, Strengthen, Thrill, Titillate,
     Uplift, Vitalise, Waken, Warm

Exclude   Ban, Banish, Bar, Boycott, Censor,
     Debar, Disallow, Disbar, Disregard,
     Disqualify, Drop, Eject, Eliminate,
     Exempt, Expel, Forbid, Ignore, Obstruct,
     Ostracise, Outlaw, Prohibit, Refuse,
     Reject, Spurn

Exculpate   Absolve, Exonerate, Forgive,
     Liberate, Pardon

Excuse   Acquit, Clear, Condone, Exempt,
     Exonerate, Forgive, Pardon, Spare,
     Vindicate

Execute   Annihilate, Destroy, Exterminate,
     Finish, Impale, Kill, Lynch, Murder,
     Shoot, Slay, Stone, Terminate

Exempt   Absolve, Acquit, Exclude, Excuse,
     Spare

Exercise   Drill, Edify, Improve

Exhaust   Debilitate, Deplete, Devitalise,
     Diminish, Disable, Drain, Empty,
     Enervate, Enfeeble, Fatigue, Impoverish,
     Incapacitate, Jade, Milk, Reduce, Sap,
     Tire, Unhinge, Weaken, Weary

Exhilarate   Animate, Boost, Brighten, Delight,
     Elate, Elevate, Enliven, Excite, Fire,
     Gladden, Hearten, Inflame, Inspire,
     Inspirit, Intoxicate, Invigorate, Lift,
     Quicken, Raise, Refresh, Revitalise,
     Rouse, Stimulate, Thrill, Uplift, Vitalise

Exhort   Force, Goad, Harangue, Harass,
     Impel, Incite, Persuade, Rally

Exile   Banish, Boycott, Dismiss, Displace,
Dispossess, Eject, Evacuate, Ostracise,
Oust

Exonerate   Absolve, Acquit, Clear, Discharge,
Exculpate, Excuse, Forgive, Liberate,
Pardon, Purge, Purify, Release, Vindicate

Expand   Boost, Distend, Inflate

Expel   Banish, Discard, Discharge, Dislodge,
Dismiss, Dispossess, Drop, Eject,
Eliminate, Evacuate, Exclude, Extrude,
Fire, Impel, Ostracise, Oust, Propel,
Reject, Spurn

Exploit   Abuse, Manipulate, Misuse, Swindle,
Use

Expose   Accuse, Confute, Detect, Rumble,
Shame, Skin, Strip, Uncover, Unmask,
Unveil

Expropriate   Deprive, Disposses

Expunge   Annihilate, Cancel, Destroy, Efface,
Erradicate, Extirpate, Obliterate

Exterminate   Annihilate, Butcher, Destroy,
Eliminate, Eradicate, Execute, Finish,
Kill, Massacre, Obliterate, Remove,
Slaughter

Extinguish   Annihilate, Cloud, Eclipse,
Eradicate, Obscure, Smother, Strangle,
Suppress

Extirpate   Annihilate, Cancel, Destroy, Efface,
Eradicate, Excise, Expunge, Obliterate

Extol   Applaud, Compliment, Emblazon,
Glorify, Laud, Praise, Proclaim, Trumpet

Extort   Compel

Extract   Draw, Pull

Extrude   Eject, Expel

Face   Confront, Encounter

Facilitate   Enable

Familiarise   Accustom, Acquaint, Coach, Habituate, Instruct, School, Season, Train

Fan   Agitate, Arouse, Excite, Provoke, Rouse, Stimulate

Fascinate   Allure, Arrest, Attract, Beguile, Bewitch, Captivate, Charm, Compel, Dazzle, Delight, Enamour, Enchant, Engage, Engross, Enrapture, Enthral, Entice, Entrance, Hold, Hypnotise, Influence, Interest, Intrigue, Mesmerise, Rivet, Tantalise

Father   Foster, Mother, Parent, Raise, Rear

Fatigue   Debilitate, Deplete, Deprive, Devitalise, Diminish, Drain, Enervate, Enfeeble, Exhaust, Harrass, Incapacitate, Jade, Sap, Tire, Unhinge, Weaken, Weary

Favour   Abet, Accommodate, Advocate, Affirm, Aid, Approve, Assist, Authorise, Aver, Back, Befriend, Boost, Champion, Confirm, Encourage, Endorse, Endow, Enrich, Forward, Foster, Grace, Gratify, Help, Honour, Indulge, Oblige, Pamper, Patronise, Promote, Ratify, Recommend, Reward, Sanction, Spoil, Strengthen, Support, Treat

Faze   Agitate, Baffle, Bewilder, Bother, Confuse, Daze, Dazzle, Disturb, Flummox, Fluster, Jumble, Muddle, Mystify, Perplex, Perturb, Puzzle, Unsettle

Feed   Augment, Bolster, Encourage, Foster, Fuel, Nourish, Nurture, Strengthen, Sustain

Felicitate   Compliment, Congratulate

F

Festoon   Adorn, Beautify, Bedeck, Deck,
        Decorate, Enrich, Ornament

Fetter   Bind, Chain, Confine, Constrain,
        Constrict, Curb, Encumber, Enslave,
        Hamper, Hold, Manacle, Pinion,
        Restrain, Restrict, Shackle, Tie, Trammel

Fiddle   Deceive, Swindle

Fight   Assault, Attack, Battle, Box, Challenge,
        Combat, Encounter, Hit

Filch   Appropriate, Misuse, Nick, Pilfer, Pinch,
        Purloin, Rob, Steal, Swipe

Fill, 1   Imbue, Replenish, Sate, Satiate, Satisfy,
        Suffuse, Swell

Fill, 2   Block, Bung, Impregnate, Plug, Stop,
        Stuff

Finish, 1   Annihilate, Defeat, Destroy, Execute,
        Exterminate, Rout, Ruin, Terminate

Finish, 2   Complete

Fire, 1   Animate, Arouse, Awaken, Blast,
        Cheer, Electrify, Embolden, Encourage,
        Enhearten, Enkindle, Enliven, Excite,
        Exhilarate, Fuel, Galvanise, Generate,
        Gladden, Hearten, Ignite, Inflame,
        Infuriate, Inspire, Inspirit, Invigorate,
        Jolt, Kindle, Launch, Light, Motivate,
        Provoke, Rouse, Quicken, Shock, Snoot,
        Stimulate, Stoke, Strengthen, Thrill,
        Trigger, Waken, Vitalise

Fire, 2   Banish, Discharge, Dislodge, Dismiss,
        Dispossess, Eject, Expel, Oust, Remove,
        Sack

Fix, 1   Affix, Anchor, Bind, Bond, Chain, Peg,
        Pin, Secure, Tie, Wedge

Fix, 2   Amend, Mend, Repair

Fixate   Captivate, Engross, Mesmerise

Flabbergast   Amaze, Astonish, Astound,
        Confound, Daze, Dazzle, Dumbfound,
        Shock, Stagger, Stun, Surprise

Flagellate   Beat, Birch, Cane, Castigate, Flog,
        Lash, Spank, Strap, Tan, Thrash, Whip

58

Flail   Beat, Thrash

Flatten   Bulldoze, Demolish, Floor, Knock, Raze, Squash, Trample

Flatter   Beguile, Butter, Cajole, Charm, Coax, Compliment, Deceive, Humour, Inveigle, Pet

Flay   Blast, Peel, Skin, Uncover

Flee   Dodge, Elude, Escape, Evade, Leave, Outrun

Fleece   Blackmail, Cheat, Defraud, Diddle, Ransack, Rob, Skin, Strip, Swindle

Flick   Flip, Hit, Jab, Peck, Rap, Tap, Toss, Touch

Fling   Chuck, Pitch, Propel, Sling, Throw, Toss

Flip   Flick, Snap, Throw, Toss, Twist

Flog   Beat, Belt, Birch, Bludgeon, Cane, Castigate, Chastise, Flagellate, Hammer, Hit, Lambast, Lash, Punch, Rap, Scourge, Slap, Slug, Smack, Smite, Sock, Strap, Tan, Thrash, Trounce, Wallop, Whack, Whip

Floor, 1   Amaze, Astonish, Astound, Baffle, Bewilder, Confound, Deck, Defeat, Discomfit, Disconcert, Dumbfound, Perplex, Puzzle, Stump, Throw

Floor, 2   Beat, Conquer, Defeat, Demolish, Fell, Flatten, Overthrow, Raze

Flummox   Baffle, Bemuse, Bewilder, Confound, Confuse, Daze, Faze, Stump, Perplex, Puzzle

Fluster   Agitate, Bother, Confuse, Discomfit, Discompose, Disconcert, Distress, Disturb, Dizzy, Embarrass, Faze, Hassle, Hurry, Panic, Perturb, Rattle, Ruffle, Unsettle, Unnerve, Upset, Vex

Focus   Centre, Concentrate, Direct, Ground

Foil, 1   Baffle, Confound, Elude, Frustrate, Outwit, Puzzle, Thwart, Parry

Foil, 2   Defeat, Nullify, Stop, Stump

Follow, 1   Accompany, Chase, Pursue, Stalk, Track, Trail

F

Follow, 2 Emulate, Serve

Fondle Caress, Cuddle, Grope, Hug,
    Manipulate, Maul, Pat, Paw, Pet, Stroke

Fool Bamboozle, Beguile, Bluff, Cheat, Con,
    Deceive, Defraud, Delude, Diddle, Dupe,
    Gull, Hoax, Hoodwink, Kid, Mislead,
    Outwit, Tease, Trick

Forbid Ban, Bar, Exclude, Debar, Disallow,
    Inhibit, Interdict, Outlaw, Preclude,
    Prohibit, Proscribe

Force Compel, Drive, Exhort, Hustle, Impel,
    Obligate, Press, Pressure, Pressurise,
    Push, Thrust, Urge, Wrench

Forestall Baffle, Block, Elude, Frustrate,
    Hinder, Parry, Stop, Stump, Thwart

Forgive Absolve, Acquit, Condone,
    Exculpate, Excuse, Exonerate, Pardon

Forsake Abandon, Betray, Desert, Discard,
    Ditch, Divorce, Drop, Dump, Jilt, Leave,
    Relinquish, Renounce, Surrender

Forward Abet, Advocate, Aid, Assist, Boost,
    Champion, Encourage, Favour, Further,
    Help, Patronise, Promote, Push, Spur,
    Strengthen, Succour, Support, Upgrade,
    Uphold, Urge

Forewarn Alert, Warn

Fortify, 1 Barricade, Harden, Inure, Protect,
    Reinforce, Secure, Strengthen, Support,
    Toughen

Fortify, 2 Cheer, Embolden, Encourage,
    Hearten, Invigorate, Reassure, Sustain

Foster Abet, Accommodate, Aid, Boost,
    Coach, Cultivate, Develop, Discipline,
    Edify, Educate, Encourage, Enlighten,
    Father, Favour, Feed, Help, Mother,
    Nourish, Nurse, Nurture, Raise, Rear,
    Support, Sustain, Teach

Foul Besmear, Contaminate, Defile, Dirty,
    Pollute, Smear, Soil, Stain, Taint

Fracture Break, Crack, Splinter, Split

Fragment Break, Crumble, Disunite, Shatter, Splinter, Split

Free Clear, Discharge, Deliver, Disencumber, Disengage, Disentangle, Disenthrall, Emancipate, Enfranchise, Liberate, Pardon, Redeem, Relieve, Release, Rescue, Unburden, Unchain, Undo, Unfetter, Unleash, Unshackle, Untie

Freeze, 1 Numb, Refrigerate

Freeze, 2 Arrest, Immobilise, Inactivate, Paralyse, Petrify, Stun

Freshen Enliven, Galvanise, Invigorate, Refresh, Restore, Revitalise, Revive, Rouse, Stimulate, Titivate, Uplift

Fret Aggravate, Agitate, Annoy, Badger, Bother, Bug, Distress, Disturb, Perturb, Pester, Provoke, Rile, Ruffle, Tease, Trouble, Upset, Vex

Frighten Affright, Alarm, Appal, Bully, Deter, Disconcert, Haunt, Horrify, Intimidate, Menace, Panic, Petrify, Scare, Shock, Spook, Startle, Terrify, Terrorise

Frisk Foil, Check, Inspect, Search

Frustrate Aggravate, Baffle, Bedevil, Confound, Confront, Cripple, Defeat, Disappoint, Elude, Escape, Foil, Forestall, Halt, Harass, Hinder, Inhibit, Neutralise, Stultify, Torment

Fuddle Bemuse, Confuse, Intoxicate

Fuel Augment, Bolster, Charge, Encourage, Feed, Fire, Incite, Inflame, Nurture, Stoke, Strengthen, Sustain

Furnish Award, Endue, Decorate, Endow, Enrich, Equip

Further Abet, Advocate, Aid, Assist, Boost, Champion, Encourage, Forward, Help, Patronise, Promote, Push, Spur, Strengthen, Succour, Support, Thrust, Upgrade

Fuse Bond, Join

Fuss Bother, Niggle

F

Gag Block, Choke, Curb, Hinder, Muffle, Mute, Muzzle, Quieten, Repress, Restrain, Silence, Stifle, Suppress, Throttle

Galvanise Activate, Animate, Arouse, Awaken, Animate, Electrify, Encourage, Enhearten, Excite, Fire, Freshen, Generate, Jolt, Incite, Inspire, Inspirit, Invigorate, Motivate, Move, Provoke, Quicken, Rouse, Shock, Spur, Startle, Stimulate, Stir, Thrill, Vitalise, Waken

Gash Cleave, Cut, Gouge, Incise, Lacerate, Slash, Slit, Tear, Wound

Gauge Appraise, Assess, Consider, Contemplate, Estimate, Evaluate, Examine, Judge, Measure, Monitor, Rank, Rate, Weigh

Generate Activate, Agitate, Arouse, Awaken, Beget, Energise, Enhearten, Enkindle, Enliven, Fire, Galvanise, Incite, Inflame, Inspire, Interest, Intrigue, Invigorate, Kindle, Move, Prompt, Provoke, Quicken, Raise, Revive, Rouse, Spark, Spur, Stimulate, Stir, Trigger, Vitalise, Waken

Gladden Amuse, Brighten, Cheer, Comfort, Content, Delight, Elate, Enliven, Exhilarate, Gratify, Hearten, Jolly, Lighten, Please

Glorify Acclaim, Aggrandise, Applaud, Bless, Dignify, Distinguish, Elevate, Emblazon, Ennoble, Exalt, Extol, Hail, Honour, Idolise, Laud, Praise, Proclaim, Revere, Sanctify, Toast, Worship

Goad Abet, Annoy, Arouse, Badger, Drive, Encourage, Energise, Exhort, Harass,

G

Hasten, Hound, Hurry, Impel, Incite,
Influence, Motivate, Persuade, Press,
Pressure, Prod, Prompt, Propel, Push,
Quicken, Rush, Spur, Stimulate, Sting,
Tease, Urge

Gouge Cleave, Cut, Gash, Hack, Incise,
Knife, Lacerate, Maul, Pick, Slash, Slit,
Split, Tear, Wound

Govern Command, Conduct, Control, Direct,
Discipline, Dominate, Domineer, Guide,
Lead, Manage, Master, Order, Rule, Steer

Grab Capture, Catch, Clutch, Embrace,
Grasp, Grip, Pluck, Pull, Seize, Snatch,
Tug, Wrench, Wrest

Grace Adorn, Beautify, Dignify, Distinguish,
Elevate, Favour

Grade Brand, Categorise, Class, Classify,
Rank, Rate, Value

Grasp Clutch, Embrace, Encircle, Grab,
Grip, Seize

Gratify Amuse, Content, Delight, Favour,
Gladden, Humour, Indulge, Please,
Pleasure, Satisfy

Greet Acknolwedge, Address, Approach,
Compliment, Hail, Receive, Recognise,
Salute, Welcome

Grill Cross-examine, Interrogate, Question,
Quiz

Grip, 1 Clasp, Clutch, Grab, Grasp

Grip, 2 Engage, Engross, Hold, Involve,
Mesmerise, Seize, Spellbind

Groom Brush, Coach, Dress, Drill, Educate,
Instruct, Nurture, Prepare, Prime,
Sophisticate, Teach, Train, Tutor

Grope Fondle, Maul, Paw

Ground Balance, Centre, Focus, Level,
Neautralise, Plant, Regulate, Root,
Secure, Settle, Stabilise, Steady

Guard Defend, Escort, Safeguard, Secure,
Shelter, Shield, Protect

Guide, 1   Advise, Coach, Counsel, Direct,
Edify, Educate, Enlighten, Govern, Help,
Improve, Influence, Inform, Instruct,
Manage, Manoeuvre, Nurture, Operate,
Rule, School, Shepherd, Steer, Teach,
Train, Tutor

Guide, 2   Conduct, Escort, Precede, Lead,
Shepherd, Usher

Gull   Bamboozle, Cheat, Con, Delude, Dupe,
Fool, Hoax, Hoodwink, Kid, Mislead,
Outwit, Swindle, Trick

G

Habituate   Accustom, Condition, Familiarise,
    Season
Hack   Chop, Cleave, Cut, Gouge, Lacerate,
    Mutilate, Slash, Wound
Hail   Acclaim, Acknowledge, Address,
    Applaud, Cheer, Exalt, Glorify, Greet,
    Honour, Praise, Salute, Welcome
Hallow   Anoint, Bless, Praise, Sanctify
Halt   Arrest, Block, Confront, Curb,
    Frustrate, Immobilise, Impede,
    Obstruct, Paralyse, Restrain, Stall, Stop
Hammer   Bang, Batter, Beat, Belt, Clobber,
    Crush, Flog, Hit, Knock, Pound,
    Pummel, Punch, Slug, Sock, Spank,
    Strike, Thump, Wallop, Whack
Hamper   Ban, Bar, Block, Burden, Chain, Clog,
    Confine, Constrain, Constrict, Cramp,
    Curb, Deter, Disrupt, Encumber, Fetter,
    Handicap, Hinder, Impair, Impede,
    Inconvenience, Limit, Obstruct, Oppress,
    Overload, Restrain, Restrict, Retard, Saddle,
    Stultify, Thwart, Tie, Trammel
Handicap   Burden, Clog, Cramp, Curb,
    Encumber, Hamper, Hinder, Impair, Impede,
    Inconvenience, Limit, Obstruct, Overload,
    Restrict, Retard, Saddle, Trammel
Harangue   Abuse, Exhort, Lash, Lecture,
    Torment
Harass   Aggravate, Agitate, Annoy,
    Antagonise, Badger, Bait, Bedevil,
    Besiege, Bombard, Bother, Browbeat,
    Bully, Chide, Criticise, Disturb, Exhort,
    Fatigue, Frustrate, Goad, Harry, Hassle,
    Heckle, Hector, Henpeck, Hound,
    Intimidate, Irritate, Nag, Needle,
    Oppress, Perplex, Persecute, Pester,

H

Plague, Provoke, Taunt, Tease, Tire,
Torment, Trouble, Upset, Vex, Worry

Harbour   Hold, Protect, Shield

Harden   Fortify, Inure, Reinforce, Steel,
Stiffen, Strengthen, Toughen

Harm   Abuse, Assault, Break, Damage, Hurt,
Impair, Injure, Maltreat, Mar, Mistreat,
Molest, Trouble, Wound, Wrong

Harmonise   Align, Heal, Compose, Reconcile,
Settle, Soothe

Harry   Annoy, Badger, Bedevil, Besiege, Bug,
Despoil, Disturb, Harass, Hassle, Hound,
Nag, Oppress, Persecute, Pester, Plague,
Pursue, Tease, Torment, Trouble, Vex

Hassle   Aggravate, Agitate, Annoy,
Antagonise, Badger, Bait, Bedevil,
Besiege, Bother, Bug, Fluster, Harass,
Harry, Hound, Nag, Niggle, Pester,
Plague, Ruffle, Tease, Torment, Trouble,
Vex, Worry

Hasten   Accelerate, Goad, Hurry, Hustle,
Press, Push, Rush, Quicken, Urge

Haunt   Curse, Disturb, Frighten, Trouble,
Urge, Worry

Hawk, 1   Attack, Hunt

Hawk, 2   Prostitute

Heal, 1   Harmonise, Reconcile, Settle, Soothe

Heal, 2   Cure, Help, Mend, Regenerate,
Remedy, Repair, Restore, Treat

Hearten   Animate, Assure, Boost, Brighten,
Cheer, Comfort, Console, Elate, Elevate,
Embolden, Encourage, Energise, Enhearten,
Enliven, Exalt, Excite, Exhilarate, Fire,
For tify, Gladden, Inflame, Inspire, Inspirit,
Invigorate, Jolly, Lift, Lighten, Nerve, Raise,
Rally, Reassure, Revitalise, Revive, Rouse,
Stimulate, Stir, Strengthen, Sustain, Uplift,
Vitalise

Heckle   Badger, Bait, Disrupt, Harass, Hector,
Jeer, Jibe, Pester, Ridicule, Taunt

Hector Aggravate, Badger, Browbeat, Bully,
Chide, Criticise, Harass, Heckle,
Henpeck, Intimidate, Jeer, Nag, Pester,
Plague, Provoke, Scold, Threaten,
Torment, Worry

Hedge Circumbscribe, Elude, Limit, Shirk

Heighten Augment, Boost, Elevate, Exalt,
Lift, Raise, Strengthen, Swell

Help Abet, Aid, Alleviate, Assist, Back,
Befriend, Boost, Encourage, Favour,
Forward, Foster, Further, Guide, Heal,
Nurse, Patronise, Promote, Relieve,
Remedy, Restore, Serve, Strengthen,
Succour, Support, Tutor

Henpeck Bully, Browbeat, Chide, Criticise,
Crowd, Harass, Hector, Intimidate, Nag,
Niggle, Pester, Scold, Torment

Hijack Capture, Ensnare, Kidnap, Pluck,
Seize, Snatch, Steal, Terrorise, Threaten

Hinder Annoy, Bar, Block, Burden, Check,
Clog, Cramp, Cripple, Curb, Debar,
Delay, Deter, Detain, Disable, Discourage,
Encumber, Forestall, Frustrate, Gag,
Hamper, Handicap, Impair, Impede,
Inconvenience, Mar, Obstruct, Oppress,
Overload, Restrain, Restrict, Retard,
Saddle, Thwart, Trammel, Wing

Hit Assault, Bang, Bash, Bat, Batter, Battle,
Beat, Belt, Box, Clip, Clobbber, Clout,
Crown, Cudgel, Cuff, Damage, Deck,
Fight, Flick, Flog, Hammer, Knock,
Punch, Rap, Slap, Slug, Smack, Smite,
Sock, Strike, Swat, Thump, Wallop,
Whack, Zap

Hoax Bamboozle, Bluff, Cheat, Con, Deceive,
Defraud, Delude, Diddle, Dupe, Entrap,
Fool, Gull, Kid, Mislead, Outwit,
Swindle, Trap, Trick

Hog Appropriate, Hold, Monopolise

Hoist Elevate, Lift, Raise, Uplift, Upraise

H

Hold, 1   Carry, Clasp, Clutch, Cradle, Cuddle, Cup, Embrace, Encompass, Enfold, Engulf, Envelop, Enwrap, Grip, Hug, Shoulder, Subsume, Support

Hold, 2   Arrest, Bind, Capture, Chain, Confine, Contain, Curb, Detain, Enclose, Enslave, Fetter, Harbour, Hog, Imprison, Manacle, Possess, Retain, Shackle, Stop

Hold, 3   Enchant, Engage, Engross, Entrance, Fascinate, Occupy, Preoccupy, Transfix

Honour   Acclaim, Admire, Aggrandise, Applaud, Award, Blazon, Commend, Compliment, Consecrate, Credit, Crown, Dignify, Distinguish, Elevate, Ennoble, Enshrine, Exalt, Favour, Glorify, Hail, Ordain, Praise, Prize, Respect, Revere, Reward, Salute, Toast, Treasure, Value, Venerate

Hoodwink   Bamboozle, Beguile, Cheat, Con, Delude, Diddle, Dupe, Fool, Gull, Kid, Mislead, Swindle, Trick

Hook   Catch, Engage, Ensnare, Entrap, Snare, Trap

Horrify   Affright, Alarm, Appal, Disgust, Frighten, Nauseate, Outrage, Petrify, Repel, Shock, Sicken, Terrify, Terrorise

Host   Entertain

Hound   Badger, Bait, Besiege, Bombard, Bully, Goad, Harass, Harry, Hassle, Hunt, Nag, Persecute, Pester, Pursue, Vex

House   Accommodate, Safeguard, Shelter, Shield

Hug   Caress, Clinch, Cuddle, Embrace, Encircle, Enclose, Encompass, Enfold, Envelop, Enwrap, Fondle, Hold, Press, Squeeze, Surround

Humble   Chasten, Crush, Debase, Deflate, Degrade, Demean, Demote, Disgrace, Downgrade, Efface, Humiliate, Lower, Reduce, Shame, Snub, Subdue

Humiliate   Belittle, Crush, Cut, Debase, Deflate, Degrade, Demean, Disgrace, Embarrass, Humble, Ridicule, Shame, Snub, Trounce

Humour   Amuse, Content, Flatter, Gratify, Indulge, Mollify, Pamper, Smooth

Hunt   Chase, Hawk, Hound, Pursue, Stalk, Track

Hurry   Accelerate, Fluster, Goad, Hasten, Hustle, Incite, Push, Quicken, Rush

Hurt   Abuse, Afflict, Aggravate, Aggrieve, Batter, Cut, Damage, Disable, Harm, Impair, Injure, Insult, Maltreat, Mar, Mistreat, Sting, Weaken, Wound, Wrong

Hush   Appease, Calm, Lull, Mollify, Mute, Muzzle, Quieten, Silence, Soothe, Stifle, Subdue, Suppress

Hustle   Bump, Crowd, Elbow, Force, Hasten, Hurry, Jostle, Move, Nudge, Push, Rush, Shove, Thrust

Hypnotise   Beguile, Bewitch, Captivate, Charm, Dazzle, Engage, Enrapture, Enthral, Entrance, Fascinate, Magnetise, Mesmerise, Rivet, Spellbind, Transfix

H

Idolise Adore, Admire, Adorn, Adulate,
    Beatify, Deify, Enshrine, Exalt, Glorify,
    Praise, Revere, Sanctify, Treasure,
    Venerate, Worship

Ignite Awaken, Brighten, Enkindle, Fire, Inflame,
    Inspire, Kindle, Light, Spark, Trigger

Ignore Boycott, Disobey, Disregard, Exclude,
    Neglect, Omit, Overlook, Reject, Snub,
    Spurn

Imbue Drench, Fill, Infuse, Saturate

Imitate Ape, Caricature, Copy, Emulate,
    Mimic, Mirror, Parody, Parrot

Immobilise Arrest, Cripple, Disable, Freeze,
    Halt, Inactivate, Incapacitate, Numb,
    Paralyse, Petrify, Pinion, Stop, Stun

Immolate Burn, Incinerate

Immortalise Beatify, Cherish, Consecrate,
    Conserve, Deify, Enshrine, Treasure

Impair Abuse, Aggravate, Blemish, Blight,
    Cloud, Contaminate, Corrupt, Cripple,
    Damage, Debase, Deface, Defile, Deform,
    Demoralise, Deplete, Deprive, Derange,
    Disable, Hamper, Handicap, Harm,
    Hinder, Hurt, Injure, Maim, Mar, Maul,
    Modify, Retard, Ruin, Sap, Spoil, Taint,
    Warp, Weaken

Impale Execute, Knife, Lance, Pierce, Prick,
    Puncture, Skewer, Spike, Stab

Impassion Arouse, Enrage, Excite, Heat,
    Inflame, Inspirit, Rouse, Stimulate, Stir,
    Warm

Impeach Accuse, Blame, Charge, Denounce,
    Disparage, Indict

Impede Ban, Bar, Block, Burden, Clog,
    Cramp, Curb, Delay, Deter, Discourage,
    Disrupt, Encumber, Halt, Hamper,

I

Handicap, Hinder, Inconvenience,
Intercept, Interdict, Interrupt, Obstruct,
Oppress, Overload, Postpone, Restrain,
Restrict, Retard, Saddle, Stop, Stultify,
Thwart, Trammel

Impel   Activate, Agitate, Animate, Compel,
Drive, Exhort, Expel, Force, Goad,
Incite, Induce, Inspire, Instigate,
Motivate, Move, Persuade, Press,
Pressurise, Prod, Prompt, Propel, Push,
Rouse, Spur, Stimulate, Urge

Imperil   Compromise, Endanger, Jeopardise,
Risk, Threaten

Implicate   Compromise, Disturb, Embroil,
Encumber, Endanger, Enmesh, Ensnare,
Entangle, Incriminate, Involve, Snare,
Trammel, Trap

Implore   Beg, Beseech, Entreat, Petition,
Press, Solicit

Importune   Beg, Entreat, Press, Solicit

Impound   Imprison, Incarcerate, Restrain,
Restrict

Impoverish   Break, Cripple, Debilitate,
Deplete, Deprive, Diminish, Drain,
Emasculate, Enervate, Exhaust, Reduce,
Ruin, Sap, Weaken

Impregnate   Fill, Infiltrate, Penetrate,
Permeate, Rape

Impress   Amaze, Arrest, Attract, Dazzle,
Interest, Move, Touch

Imprison   Cage, Detain, Hold, Impound,
Incarcerate, Restrain, Trap

Improve   Aid, Amend, Assist, Better, Beautify,
Boost, Civilise, Coach, Correct,
Cultivate, Cure, Develop, Edify, Educate,
Elevate, Emend, Enlighten, Exercise,
Guide, Modify, Nurture, Polish, Refine,
Reform, Reinforce, Remedy, School,
Sharpen, Strengthen, Teach, Train, Tutor,
Upgrade

Impugn   Abuse, Accost, Assail, Assault,
        Attack, Berate, Blacken, Blast, Censure,
        Slander
Inactivate   Freeze, Immobilise, Numb, Stop
Incapacitate   Break, Cripple, Debilitate,
        Deprive, Devitalise, Disable, Drain,
        Enervate, Enfeeble, Exhaust, Fatigue,
        Immobilise, Paralyse, Restrict, Sabotage,
        Sap, Tire, Unnerve, Weaken
Incarcerate   Cage, Impound, Imprison,
        Restrain, Restrict
Incense   Antagonise, Enrage, Exasperate,
        Inflame, Infuriate, Madden, Outrage, Vex
Incinerate   Burn, Destroy, Immolate
Incise   Cleave, Cut, Gash, Gouge, Lacerate,
        Slash, Slit, Split, Tear, Wound
Incite   Agitate, Animate, Arouse, Awaken,
        Beget, Call, Embolden, Encourage,
        Enkindle, Enrage, Excite, Exhort, Fuel,
        Galvanise, Generate, Goad, Hurry, Impel,
        Induce, Inflame, Influence, Inspire,
        Inspirit, Instigate, Invigorate, Kindle,
        Motivate, Persuade, Prod, Propel,
        Provoke, Quicken, Rally, Rouse, Spark,
        Spur, Stimulate, Stir, Urge
Include   Encompass, Enjoin, Incorporate,
        Integrate, Involve
Inconvenience   Bother, Burden, Encumber,
        Hamper, Handicap, Hinder, Impede,
        Overload, Retard, Saddle, Trammel
Incorporate   Absorb, Embrace, Encompass,
        Enjoin, Include, Integrate, Join, Subsume
Incriminate   Accuse, Blame, Charge,
        Implicate, Involve
Indict   Accuse, Arraign, Attack, Ban, Blame,
        Charge, Denounce, Impeach, Prohibit,
        Prosecute
Indoctrinate   Brainwash, Coach, Condition,
        Convert, Discipline, Drill, Edify, Educate,
        School, Teach, Train, Tutor

I

Induce   Allure, Attract, Beguile, Bribe,
Ensnare, Entice, Entrap, Impel, Incite,
Lure, Motivate, Persuade, Seduce, Tempt

Induct   Initiate

Indulge   Appease, Favour, Gratify, Humour,
Mollycoddle, Pamper, Placate, Please,
Pleasure, Regale, Reward, Satisfy, Spoil,
Tolerate

Inebriate   Intoxicate, Stupefy, Unbalance, Unhinge

Infect   Blight, Contaminate, Corrupt, Excite,
Influence, Poison, Pollute, Taint

Infest   Attack, Invade, Overload, Overwhelm,
Penetrate, Swamp

Infiltrate   Impregnate, Invade, Penetrate,
Permeate

Inflame   Aggravate, Agitate, Animate, Arouse,
Awaken, Embolden, Encourage,
Enkindle, Enrage, Excite, Exhilarate,
Fire, Fuel, Generate, Hearten, Ignite,
Impassion, Incense, Incite, Infuriate,
Inspire, Inspirit, Intoxicate, Invigorate,
Kindle, Light, Madden, Nerve, Rouse,
Stimulate, Stir, Stoke, Strengthen, Vitalise

Inflate   Aggrandise, Augment, Boost, Distend,
Expand, Swell

Influence   Affect, Encourage, Fascinate, Goad,
Guide, Incite, Infect, Inspire, Manage,
Manipulate, Motivate, Operate,
Permeate, Steer, Tempt, Urge, Work

Inform, 1   Acquaint, Advise, Apprise, Brief,
Civilise, Counsel, Edify, Educate, Elevate,
Enlighten, Guide, Instruct, Notify

Inform, 2   Coach, Cultivate, Debrief,
Discipline, Drill, Influence, Instruct,
Nurture, School, Teach, Train, Tutor

Infuriate   Enrage, Exasperate, Fire, Incense,
Inflame, Madden, Outrage, Rile, Rouse, Vex

Infuse   Drench, Imbue, Saturate, Soak,
Suffuse

Inhabit   Occupy, Possess

Inhibit   Block, Constrain, Cramp, Curb,
Detain, Discourage, Forbid, Frustrate,
Obstruct, Prohibit, Restrain, Stop

Initiate   Activate, Admit, Induct

Injure   Abuse, Batter, Break, Bruise, Cripple,
Damage, Deface, Harm, Hurt, Impair,
Insult, Maltreat, Mar, Mistreat, Ruin,
Spoil, Weaken, Wound, Wrong

Inoculate   Protect, Safeguard

Inspect   Frisk, Investigate, Scrutinise, Search

Inspire   Animate, Arouse, Awaken, Brighten,
Cheer, Embolden, Encourage, Enhearten,
Enkindle, Enliven, Excite, Exhilarate,
Fire, Galvanise, Generate, Hearten,
Heat, Ignite, Impel, Incite, Inflame,
Influence, Inspirit, Invigorate, Kindle,
Motivate, Propel, Provoke, Rally, Rouse,
Spark, Spur, Stimulate, Stir, Vitalise

Inspirit   Activate, Animate, Assure, Brighten,
Cheer, Electrify, Embolden, Encourage,
Energise, Enhearten, Enliven, Excite,
Exhilarate, Fire, Galvanise, Hearten, Heat,
Impassion, Incite, Inflame, Inspire,
Invigorate, Motivate, Nerve, Raise, Rally,
Reassure, Regenerate, Revive, Rouse,
Stimulate, Stir, Strengthen, Uplift, Vitalise

Instruct   Advise, Apprise, Bid, Civilise, Coach,
Command, Compel, Counsel, Cultivate,
Develop, Discipline, Drill, Edify, Educate,
Elevate, Enlighten, Familiarise, Groom,
Guide, Inform, Lecture, Order, School,
Teach, Train, Tutor

Insulate   Protect, Safeguard

Insult   Abuse, Affront, Antagonise, Bruise,
Curse, Cuss, Degrade, Denigrate, Hurt,
Injure, Jeer, Mock, Offend, Outrage,
Slander, Slight, Snub, Taunt, Wound

Insure   Protect, Safeguard

Instigate   Activate, Energise, Impel, Incite,
Motivate, Prompt, Quicken, Stimulate

I

Intercept   Block, Deflect, Divert, Impede,
   Obstruct, Stop

Interdict   Ban, Banish, Bar, Block, Forbid,
   Impede, Prohibit, Restrict, Stop

Interest   Affect, Arm, Arouse, Divert, Engage,
   Engross, Fascinate, Generate, Impress,
   Intrigue, Involve

Interrogate   Catechise, Challenge,
   Cross–examine, Grill, Interview, Probe,
   Pump, Question, Quiz

Interview   Cross–examine, Interrogate,
   Question, Quiz

Interrupt   Disrupt, Impede

Integrate   Include, Incorporate

Intimidate   Blackmail, Brutalise, Bully, Chide,
   Deter, Dishearten, Dispirit, Frighten,
   Harass, Hector, Henpeck, Menace, Repress,
   Terrorise, Threaten, Torment, Tyrannise

Intoxicate   Arouse, Excite, Exhilarate, Fuddle,
   Inebriate, Inflame, Invigorate, Unbalance

Intrigue   Arouse, Attract, Captivate, Charm,
   Entertain, Enthral, Fascinate, Generate,
   Interest, Rivet

Inundate   Swamp

Inure   Fortify, Harden, Reinforce, Strengthen

Invade   Assail, Assault, Attack, Infest, Infiltrate,
   Penetrate, Permeate, Raid, Ravage

Invalidate   Cancel, Debilitate, Disable,
   Negate, Nullify, Override, Overrule,
   Revoke, Undercut, Weaken

Inveigle   Allure, Beguile, Cajole, Charm,
   Coax, Con, Court, Decoy, Entice, Entrap,
   Flatter, Lure

Investigate   Analyse, Cross–examine, Inspect,
   Probe, Question, Scrutinise

Invigorate   Activate, Animate, Arouse, Boost,
   Brighten, Cheer, Electrify, Embolden,
   Encourage, Energise, Enkindle, Enliven,
   Excite, Exhilarate, Fire, Fortify, Freshen,
   Galvanise, Generate, Hearten, Incite,

Inflame, Inspire, Inspirit, Intoxicate, Jolt,
Kindle, Motivate, Nerve, Promote,
Quicken, Reassure, Refresh, Regenerate,
Rejuvenate, Revive, Rouse, Shock,
Stiffen, Stimulate, Stir, Strengthen,
Sustain, Uplift, Vitalise

Invite   Attract, Beckon, Welcome

Invoke   Address, Conjure, Petition, Summon

Involve   Admit, Embroil, Encompass,
Encumber, Engage, Engross, Engulf,
Enmesh, Ensnare, Entangle, Entrance,
Grip, Implicate, Include, Incorporate,
Incriminate, Interest, Preoccupy

Irk   Aggravate, Annoy, Antagonise, Bait,
Bedevil, Displease, Irritate, Needle,
Peeve, Pester, Plague, Provoke, Rile,
Ruffle, Vex, Weary

Irritate   Aggravate, Annoy, Antagonise, Bait,
Bedevil, Exasperate, Harass, Irk, Madden,
Nag, Nark, Needle, Nettle, Niggle, Peeve,
Pester, Plague, Provoke, Rattle, Rile,
Tease, Torment, Vex

Isolate (PL)   Detach, Disconnect, Maroon,
Segregate, Separate

I

Jab Bump, Dig, Elbow, Flick, Knock, Nudge,
Poke, Prod, Punch, Touch

Jade Devitalise, Disappoint, Drain, Enervate,
Enfeeble, Exhaust, Fatigue, Sap, Tire,
Weary

Jeer Abuse, Bait, Heckle, Hector, Insult, Jibe,
Mock, Pester, Ridicule, Taunt

Jeopardise Imperil, Threaten, Terrorise

Jibe Heckle, Jeer, Ridicule, Tarnish, Taunt

Jilt Abandon, Betray, Desert, Ditch, Drop,
Forsake, Leave, Reject, Relinquish

Join (PL) Ally, Entwine, Fuse, Incorporate,
Link, Marry, Match

Jolly Cheer, Gladden, Hearten

Jolt Amaze, Astonish, Electrify, Excite, Fire,
Galvanise, Invigorate, Rouse, Shake,
Shock, Startle, Stimulate, Stir

Jostle Bump, Crowd, Elbow, Hustle, Nudge,
Push, Shove

Judge, 1 Analyse, Appraise, Consider, Gauge,
Measure

Judge, 2 Adjudicate, Arbitrate, Assess,
Referee, Try, Umpire

Jumble Agitate, Befuddle, Confuse, Faze,
Muddle, Perplex

J

Kick Boot

Kid Beguile, Delude, Fool, Gull, Hoax, Hoodwink, Mock, Ridicule, Tease, Trick

Kidnap Abduct, Capture, Hijack, Seize

Kill Annihilate, Butcher, Destroy, Eliminate, Eradicate, Execute, Exterminate, Lynch, Murder, Sacrifice, Slay, Terminate, Zap

Kindle Arouse, Awaken, Burn, Enkindle, Excite, Fire, Generate, Ignite, Incite, Inflame, Inspire, Invigorate, Light, Rekindle, Spark, Stoke, Waken

Kiss Brush, Caress, Peck, Touch

Knife Cut, Gouge, Impale, Pierce, Skewer, Slash, Slit, Stab, Wound

Knight Compliment, Dignify, Recognise, Reward, Salute

Knock, 1 Attack, Bang, Beat, Bump, Clobber, Cudgel, Cuff, Defame, Demolish, Elbow, Flatten, Hammer, Hit, Jab, Lambast, Nudge, Punch, Push, Rap, Shove, Slug, Sock, Wallop

Knock, 2 Abuse, Attack, Belittle, Berate, Censure, Criticise, Rebuff, Slander

K

Label   Class, Mark

Lacerate   Cleave, Cut, Gash, Gouge, Hack, Incise, Rip, Slash, Slit, Tear, Wound

Lambast   Beat, Berate, Bludgeon, Castigate, Censure, Clobber, Flog, Knock, Rebuke, Reprimand, Scold, Sock, Whack

Lampoon   Satirise

Lance   Cut, Impale, Pierce

Lash, 1   Attack, Batter, Beat, Flagellate, Flog, Harangue, Strike, Tan, Whip

Lash, 2   Secure, Strap, Tie

Laud   Acclaim, Admire, Adulate, Applaud, Compliment, Emblazon, Extol, Glorify, Praise, Revere, Trumpet

Launch   Fire, Galvanise, Propel, Shoot

Lead   Accompany, Conduct, Direct, Escort, Govern, Guide, Motivate, Precede, Shepherd, Steer, Usher

Leave   Abandon, Desert, Discard, Drop, Flee, Forsake, Jilt, Relinquish, Renounce

Lecture, 1   Censure, Chide, Harangue, Reprimand, Reprove, Scold, Tutor

Lecture, 2   Instruct, Teach

Legitimise   Authorise

Lessen   Alleviate, Calm, Deprive, Diminish, Lower, Reduce, Subordinate, Weaken

Level   Balance, Ground, Smooth, Steady

Liberate   Absolve, Acquit, Deliver, Demobilise, Discharge, Disencumber, Disengage, Disentangle, Disenthrall, Emancipate, Enfranchise, Exculpate, Exonerate, Free, Pardon, Redeem, Release, Rescue, Save, Spare, Unburden, Unchain, Unfetter, Unshackle, Unleash, Untie

L

License   Authorise, Commission, Empower,
        Enable, Entitle, Permit, Qualify, Sanction,
        Warrant

Lick   Caress

Lift   Boost, Elevate, Encourage, Exalt,
        Exhilarate, Hearten, Heighten, Hoist,
        Lighten, Raise, Revive, Swell, Uplift

Light   Enliven, Fire, Ignite, Inflame, Kindle,
        Trigger

Lighten   Allay, Alleviate, Assuage, Calm,
        Cheer, Clear, Disburden, Ease, Gladden,
        Hearten, Lift, Relax, Relieve, Soothe,
        Tranquillise

Limit   Categorise, Confine, Cramp,
        Demarcate, Hamper, Handicap, Hedge,
        Restrict

Link (PL)   Entwine, Join

Lobby   Pressurise

Locate   Orientate, Place

Lock   Chain, Secure, Tie

Lodge   Accommodate, Wedge

Lower   Cheapen, Debase, Diminish,
        Downgrade, Efface, Humble, Lessen,
        Reduce, Subordinate

Lull   Allay, Assuage, Calm, Cradle, Hush,
        Pacify, Quell, Quieten, Relieve, Settle,
        Silence, Soothe, Tranquillise

Lure   Allure, Attract, Bait, Beckon, Beguile,
        Cajole, Con, Ensnare, Entice, Entrap,
        Induce, Inveigle, Magnetise, Seduce,
        Tempt

Lynch   Execute, Kill, Murder

Madden   Annoy, Enrage, Incense, Inflame,
Infuriate, Irritate, Outrage, Provoke,
Unhinge, Upset

Magnetise   Attract, Hypnotise, Lure,
Mesmerise, Pull, Rivet

Maim   Cripple, Damage, Disable, Impair,
Mangle, Mar, Wound

Malign   Abuse, Attack, Blacken, Defame,
Slander

Maltreat   Abuse, Aggravate, Damage, Harm,
Hurt, Injure, Mishandle, Mistreat,
Misuse, Molest, Persecute, Torment,
Wound, Wrong

Manacle   Chain, Confine, Encumber, Enslave,
Fetter, Hold, Pinion, Shackle

Manage   Conduct, Control, Direct, Govern,
Guide, Influence, Manipulate,
Manoeuvre, Operate, Organise, Police,
Steer, Work

Mangle   Butcher, Cripple, Crush, Destroy,
Distort, Maim, Maul, Mutilate, Wreck

Manhandle   Abuse, Molest

Manipulate, 1   Fondle, Massage, Maul, Touch

Manipulate, 2   Control, Engineer, Exploit,
Influence, Manage, Manoeuvre, Operate,
Steer, Trick, Work

Manoeuvre   Conduct, Control, Direct,
Engineer, Guide, Manage, Manipulate,
Navigate, Steer

Mar   Abuse, Blight, Blemish, Damage, Deface,
Harm, Hinder, Hurt, Impair, Injure,
Maim, Scar, Spoil, Taint, Tarnish

Mark, 1   Label

Mark, 2   Brand, Scar

Marry   Espouse, Join, Wed

Maroon   Desert, Isolate

M

Mash   Crush, Mince, Squash

Massacre   Annihilate, Butcher, Exterminate, Slaughter

Massage   Caress, Curb, Manipulate, Mould, Relax, Rub, Stroke, Touch

Master   Command, Control, Dominate, Govern, Overpower, Overcome, Repress, Rule, Subdue, Vanquish

Match   Equal, Join, Parry

Mature   Sophisticate

Maul   Attack, Batter, Beat, Fondle, Gouge, Grope, Impair, Mangle, Manipulate, Savage, Wound

Measure   Appraise, Assess, Calculate, Consider, Contemplate, Estimate, Evaluate, Gauge, Judge, Weigh

Mediate   Adjudicate, Arbitrate, Umpire

Mellow   Subdue

Melt   Defrost, Disarm, Dissolve, Warm

Menace   Affright, Alarm, Bully, Frighten, Intimidate, Scare, Terrorise, Threaten

Mend   Amend, Better, Cure, Fix, Heal, Reassemble, Regenerate, Remedy, Repair, Restore, Treat

Mesmerise   Beguile, Bewitch, Captivate, Charm, Compel, Enamour, Enchant, Engage, Enrapture, Enthral, Entrance, Fascinate, Fixate, Grip, Hypnotise, Magnetise, Spellbind, Transfix

Milk   Deflate, Drain, Exhaust

Mimic   Caricature, Copy, Emulate, Imitate, Parody, Parrot

Mince   Mash, Pulverise

Mirror   Ape, Copy, Echo, Imitate, Parrot, Reflect

Misdirect   Deflect, Misguide, Mislead

Misemploy   Abuse

Misguide   Bluff, Deceive, Delude, Misdirect, Mislead

Mishandle   Maltreat, Mistreat

Misjudge   Underestimate

Mislead   Beguile, Bluff, Deceive, Delude, Fool, Gull, Hoax, Hoodwink, Misdirect, Misguide, Pervert, Trick

Mistreat   Abuse, Brutalise, Damage, Harm, Hurt, Injure, Maltreat, Mishandle, Misuse, Molest

Misuse   Abuse, Appropriate, Exploit, Filch, Maltreat, Mistreat, Pervert, Use

Mob   Assault, Charge, Overwhelm, Pursue

Mobilise   Activate, Animate

Mock   Deride, Insult, Jeer, Kid, Pan, Patronise, Ridicule, Satirise, Shame, Slight, Taunt, Tease

Moderate   Control, Correct, Curb, Regulate, Temper, Weaken

Modify   Affect, Alter, Amend, Contort, Impair, Improve, Pervert, Reform, Twist, Warp, Weaken

Molest   Abuse, Afflict, Assault, Debauch, Deflower, Harm, Maltreat, Manhandle, Mistreat, Persecute, Rape

M

Mollify   Appease, Assuage, Calm, Comfort, Conciliate, Content, Disburden, Ease, Humour, Hush, Pacify, Placate, Propitiate, Quell, Quieten, Relax, Soothe, Sweeten, Temper

Mollycoddle   Coddle, Cosset, Indulge, Pamper, Pet, Spoil

Monitor   Gauge

Monopolise   Corner, Dominate, Engross, Hog

Mortify   Distress

Motivate   Activate, Animate, Compel, Direct, Drive, Electrify, Encourage, Energise, Enliven, Excite, Fire, Galvanise, Goad, Impel, Incite, Induce, Influence, Inspire, Inspirit, Instigate, Invigorate, Lead, Prod, Provoke, Push, Quicken, Spur, Stimulate, Urge, Vitalise

Mother   Father, Foster, Nurture, Parent

Mould   Discipline, Educate, Massage, Sculpt, Shape

Move, 1   Animate, Arouse, Galvanise, Generate, Hustle, Impel, Impress, Propel, Pull, Stimulate, Stir, Tug

Move, 2   Affect, Influence, Touch

Muddle   Befuddle, Bemuse, Cloud, Confound, Confuse, Derange, Distract, Disturb, Embroil, Entangle, Faze, Jumble, Perplex, Perturb, Trouble

Muffle   Cover, Cushion, Deaden, Gag, Mute, Muzzle, Quieten, Repress, Smother, Silence, Strangle, Stifle, Suppress, Wrap

Mug   Assault, Attack, Rob

Murder   Annihilate, Destroy, Eliminate, Execute, Kill, Lynch, Slaughter, Slay, Terminate

Mute   Cover, Dampen, Hush, Gag, Muffle, Muzzle, Silence, Stifle, Stop

Mutilate   Butcher, Cripple, Damage, Deform, Dismember, Hack, Mangle

Muzzle   Curb, Gag, Hush, Muffle, Mute Quieten, Silence, Stifle, Stop, Suppress

Mystify   Amaze, Astonish, Baffle, Bamboozle, Befuddle, Bewilder, Confound, Confuse, Enchant, Faze, Perplex, Puzzle, Stump

Nab   Arrest, Capture, Ensnare, Net, Nick, Pluck, Snatch

Nag   Annoy, Badger, Besiege, Browbeat, Bully, Chastise, Chide, Criticise, Harass, Harry, Hassle, Hector, Henpeck, Hound, Irritate, Nark, Needle, Nettle, Niggle, Pester, Plague, Provoke, Ruffle, Scold, Torment, Vex

Nail   Arrest, Capture, Catch, Seize

Name   Address, Baptise, Call, Class

Nark   Aggravate, Annoy, Antagonise, Bait, Irritate, Nag, Needle, Rile, Upset, Vex

Nauseate   Disgust, Horrify, Offend, Repel, Repulse, Sicken

Navigate   Direct, Manoeuvre, Steer, Usher

Needle,   Aggravate, Annoy, Bait, Harass, Irk, Irritate, Nag, Nark, Nettle, Niggle, Pester, Prick, Prod, Provoke, Rile, Ruffle, Sting, Taunt, Tease

N

Negate   Annihilate, Confute, Contradict, Invalidate, Nullify, Prohibit

Neglect   Avoid, Desert, Disregard, Ignore, Rebuff

Nerve   Animate, Embolden, Encourage, Hearten, Inflame, Inspirit, Invigorate, Reassure, Rouse, Stimulate, Stir, Strengthen, Vitalise

Net   Capture, Ensnare, Entangle, Entrap, Nab, Trap

Nettle   Aggravate, Annoy, Irritate, Nag, Needle, Plague, Ruffle, Vex

Neutralise   Ground, Normalise

Nibble   Nip, Peck

Nick, 1   Chip, Cut, Damage, Scratch, Wound

Nick, 2   Arrest, Capture, Nab

Nick, 3   Steal, Filch, Pinch, Pilfer, Purloin, Swipe

Niggle   Annoy, Fuss, Hassle, Henpeck,
      Irritate, Nag, Needle, Pester, Worry

Nip   Bite, Nibble, Pinch

Nominate   Appoint, Assign, Choose,
      Designate, Pick, Select

Normalise   Demobilise, Neutralise,
      Regularise, Stabilise

Notch   Cut, Chip

Notify   Advise, Alert, Inform, Warn

Nourish   Boost, Comfort, Encourage, Feed,
      Foster, Nurse, Nurture, Support, Sustain,
      Wean

Nudge   Bump, Crowd, Elbow, Hustle, Jab,
      Jostle, Knock, Poke, Prod, Push, Remind,
      Shoulder, Shove

Nullify   Abolish, Annihilate, Defeat, Destroy,
      Foil, Invalidate, Negate, Renounce,
      Rescind

Numb   Anaesthetise, Arrest, Chill, Deaden,
      Dull, Freeze, Immobilise, Inactivate,
      Paralyse, Stultify, Stun, Stupefy

Nurse   Aid, Assist, Boost, Encourage, Foster,
      Help, Nourish, Nurture, Support

Nurture, 1   Cultivate, Edify, Educate, Elevate,
      Encourage, Enlighten, Foster, Groom,
      Guide, Improve, Inform, School, Sustain,
      Teach, Train, Uplift

Nurture, 2   Bolster, Cherish, Feed, Fuel,
      Mother, Nourish, Nurse, Raise, Rear,
      Strengthen, Support, Sustain, Strengthen,
      Touch, Wean

Nuzzle   Caress, Embrace

Obey   Abide, Oblige, Serve

Obligate   Commit, Compel, Constrain, Enforce, Engage, Excise, Force, Oblige

Oblige, 1   Accommodate, Favour, Obey, Pledge, Serve

Oblige, 2   Compel, Enforce, Obligate

Obliterate   Annihilate, Cancel, Censor, Demolish, Destroy, Efface, Eradicate, Expunge, Exterminate, Extirpate, Raze, Submerge

Obscure   Cloud, Dim, Eclipse, Extinguish, Overshadow, Shroud, Veil

Observe   Study

Obstruct   Arrest, Bar, Barricade, Block, Burden, Choke, Clog, Confront, Curb, Debar, Deflect, Deter, Discourage, Divert, Encumber, Exclude, Halt, Hamper, Handicap, Hinder, Impede, Inhibit, Intercept, Parry, Prohibit, Retard, Resist, Stop, Stultify, Thwart, Trammel

Obtain   Enlist, Possess

Occupy   Engage, Engross, Hold, Inhabit, Preoccupy, Retain

Offend   Bruise, Disgust, Displease, Insult, Nauseate, Outrage, Repel, Repulse, Sicken, Slight, Snub, Upset

Operate   Guide, Influence, Manage, Manipulate, Steer, Work

Oppose   Challenge, Contradict, Discourage, Rebuff

Oppress   Afflict, Bully, Burden, Clog, Cramp, Crush, Curb, Depress, Discourage, Dishearten, Dispirit, Encumber, Hamper, Harass, Harry, Hinder, Impede, Overload, Overpower, Overwhelm, Persecute, Plague, Repress, Saddle, Squeeze, Stress,

O

Subdue, Suppress, Terrorise, Trammel,
Trample, Tyrannise, Victimise

Ordain   Anoint, Appoint, Commission,
Consecrate, Honour

Order   Classify, Command, Control, Govern,
Instruct, Police, Regulate

Organise   Control, Manage

Orientate   Direct, Locate, Place

Ornament   Adorn, Beautify, Bedeck, Deck,
Decorate, Emblazon, Enrich, Festoon

Ostracise   Avoid, Banish, Boycott, Exclude,
Exile, Expel, Prohibit, Shun, Snub

Oust   Banish, Depose, Discard, Discharge,
Dislodge, Dismiss, Dispossess, Eject,
Evacuate, Exile, Expel, Fire, Sack

Outbid   Outdo

Outdo   Better, Defeat, Eclipse, Exceed,
Outbid, Outwit, Outshine, Outsmart,
Surpass, Top, Transcend, Trump

Outlaw   Ban, Banish, Condemn, Exclude,
Forbid, Prohibit

Outrage   Affront, Antagonise, Disgust,
Enrage, Horrify, Incense, Infuriate,
Insult, Madden, Offend, Scandalise,
Shock, Slander

Outrun   Dodge, Elude, Escape, Evade, Flee,
Shun, Sidestep

Outshine   Eclipse, Exceed, Outdo, Surpass,
Top, Transcend

Outsmart   Better, Outdo, Outwit, Top, Trap,
Trip, Trump

Outstrip   Beat, Better

Outwit   Baffle, Beat, Cheat, Confound,
Delude, Dupe, Elude, Foil, Fool, Gull,
Hoax, Outdo, Outsmart, Stump, Thwart,
Top, Trap, Trick, Trip, Trump

Overcome   Conquer, Master, Overwhelm,
Prostrate, Repress, Surmount

Overhaul   Repair, Restore

Overload   Burden, Clog, Encumber, Hamper,
        Handicap, Hinder, Impede,
        Inconvenience, Infest, Oppress, Retard,
        Saddle, Trammel
Overlook   Disregard, Ignore, Snub
Overmaster   Capture, Conquer, Crush,
        Dominate, Domineer, Overpower,
        Suppress, Vanquish
Overpower   Conquer, Crush, Dazzle, Defeat,
        Dominate, Domineer, Master, Oppress,
        Overmaster, Overwhelm, Quash, Quell,
        Repress, Suppress, Vanquish
Override   Displace, Invalidate
Overrule   Invalidate, Revoke
Overshadow   Eclipse, Obscure, Shroud
Overthrow   Abolish, Conquer, Crush, Defeat,
        Demolish, Depose, Dethrone, Overturn,
        Topple
Overturn   Demolish, Overthrow,
        Revolutionise
Overwhelm   Beat, Conquer, Consume, Crush,
        Dazzle, Defeat, Deluge, Engulf, Envelop,
        Infest, Mob, Oppress, Overcome,
        Overpower, Quash, Subdue, Submerge,
        Swamp, Vanquish
Own   Appropriate, Claim, Possess

O

Pacify   Allay, Appease, Assuage, Calm,
Comfort, Conciliate, Disburden, Ease,
Lull, Mollify, Placate, Propitiate, Quell,
Quieten, Reconcile, Relax, Relieve, Satisfy,
Settle, Soothe, Sweeten, Tranquillise
Pamper   Cosset, Favour, Humour, Indulge,
Mollycoddle, Pet, Spoil, Treat
Pan   Criticise, Dispraise, Mock, Scorn
Panic   Agitate, Alarm, Fluster, Frighten,
Scare, Terrify, Unnerve
Paralyse   Anaesthetise, Arrest, Benumb,
Cripple, Deaden, Debilitate, Devitalise,
Disable, Enervate, Enfeeble, Freeze, Halt,
Immobilise, Incapacitate, Numb, Petrify,
Sap, Stun, Terrify, Transfix, Unnerve
Pardon   Absolve, Acquit, Discharge,
Exculpate, Excuse, Exonerate, Forgive,
Free, Liberate
Parent   Father, Mother
Parody   Caricature, Imitate, Mimic, Satirise
Parrot   Ape, Copy, Echo, Imitate, Mimic, Mirror
Parry   Avert, Avoid, Beg, Evade, Foil, Forestall,
Match, Obstruct, Resist, Stall, Thwart

P

Pat   Caress, Dab, Fondle, Paw, Stroke, Tap,
Touch
Patronise, 1   Abet, Advocate, Befriend,
Champion, Encourage, Favour, Forward,
Further, Help, Promote, Protect, Push,
Support
Patronise, 2   Belittle, Degrade, Mock
Paw   Caress, Fondle, Maul, Pat, Stroke, Touch
Pay   Recompense, Remunerate, Reward
Peck   Flick, Kiss, Nibble, Touch
Peel   Flay, Skin
Peeve   Annoy, Irk, Irritate
Peg   Fix, Pin, Secure

Pelt   Assail, Batter, Beat, Bombard, Pummel, Strike, Thrash, Throw, Wallop

Pen   Circumscribe, Confine, Enclose

Penetrate   Broach, Impregnate, Infest, Infiltrate, Invade, Permeate, Pierce, Prick, Probe, Ravage, Stab

Perfect   Crown, Cultivate, Develop, Refine

Perforate   Pierce, Prick, Puncture, Stab

Permeate   Assail, Impregnate, Infiltrate, Influence, Invade, Penetrate

Permit   Accept, Admit, Approve, Authorise, Empower, Enable, Endorse, Entitle, License, Qualify, Sanction, Validate, Warrant

Perplex   Baffle, Befuddle, Bemuse, Bewilder, Confound, Confuse, Daze, Disturb, Dumbfound, Faze, Floor, Flummox, Harass, Jumble, Mystify, Muddle, Puzzle, Stump, Trouble

Persecute   Abuse, Afflict, Attack, Badger, Bait, Bully, Harass, Harry, Hound, Maltreat, Molest, Oppress, Plague, Pursue, Torment, Torture, Tyrannise, Vex, Victimise, Worry

Persuade   Allure, Assure, Cajole, Coax, Convince, Encourage, Entice, Exhort, Goad, Impel, Incite, Induce, Press, Prod, Rouse, Urge, Win

Perturb   Agitate, Alarm, Bother, Concern, Confuse, Derange, Discomfit, Discomfort, Discompose, Disconcert, Displease, Disquiet, Disturb, Faze, Fluster, Fret, Muddle, Ruffle, Trouble, Unnerve, Unsettle, Upset, Vex, Worry

Peruse   Examine, Study

Pervert   Abuse, Bend, Contort, Corrupt, Debase, Debauch, Deform, Degrade, Dehumanise, Deprave, Derange, Desecrate, Deviate, Distort, Mislead, Misuse, Modify, Transform, Turn, Twist, Warp

Pester   Aggravate, Annoy, Badger, Bait, Bedevil, Besiege, Bother, Browbeat, Bully, Disturb, Fret, Harass, Harry, Hassle, Henpeck, Hound, Irk, Irritate, Jeer, Nag, Needle, Niggle, Plague, Taunt, Tease, Torment, Trouble, Vex, Worry

Pet   Caress, Cherish, Cradle, Cuddle, Flatter, Fondle, Mollycoddle, Pamper, Spoil, Stroke, Treasure

Petition   Entreat, Implore, Invoke

Petrify, 1   Alarm, Anaesthetise, Frighten, Horrify, Scare, Stun, Terrify, Terrorise

Petrify, 2   Freeze, Immobilise, Paralyse, Transfix

Pick, 1   Appoint, Choose, Designate, Elect, Nominate, Select

Pick, 2   Gouge, Pull, Scratch

Pierce   Broach, Cut, Drill, Impale, Knife, Lance, Penetrate, Perforate, Prick, Puncture, Slit, Skewer, Spike, Stab

Pigeonhole   Box, Constrain, Limit, Trap

Pilfer   Filch, Nick, Purloin, Rob, Steal

Pillage   Despoil, Rob, Sack

Pimp   Prostitute, Sell

Pin   Affix, Fix, Peg, Secure

Pinch, 1   Filch, Nick, Purloin, Rob, Steal, Swipe

Pinch, 2   Nip, Squeeze

Pinion   Bind, Chain, Confine, Enslave, Fetter, Immobilise, Manacle, Shackle, Tie

Placate   Allay, Appease, Assuage, Calm, Conciliate, Content, Indulge, Mollify, Pacify, Please, Propitiate, Reconcile, Satisfy, Soothe

Place   Accommodate, Allocate, Locate, Orientate

Plague   Annoy, Badger, Bedevil, Besiege, Bug, Curse, Cuss, Disturb, Harass, Harry, Hassle, Hector, Irk, Irritate, Nag, Nettle, Oppress, Persecute, Pester, Terrorise, Torment, Trouble, Vex, Weary, Worry

P

Plant   Embed, Ground, Root

Please   Amuse, Charm, Cheer, Content, Delight, Gladden, Gratify, Indulge, Placate, Pleasure, Satisfy

Pleasure   Delight, Gratify, Indulge, Please

Pledge   Commit, Oblige

Pluck   Abduct, Capture, Catch, Clutch, Grab, Hijack, Nab, Remove, Seize, Snatch

Plunder   Appropriate, Demolish, Destroy, Devastate, Ransack, Ravage, Rob, Shatter, Wreck

Plunge   Douse, Drown

Poison   Alienate, Befoul, Contaminate, Corrupt, Disaffect, Embitter, Envenom, Infect, Pollute, Sour, Taint, Vitiate

Poke   Jab, Nudge, Probe, Prod, Push, Shove, Taunt, Tease

Police   Manage, Order, Regulate, Restrain, Rule, Safeguard

Polish   Civilise, Cultivate, Emend, Improve, Refine

Pollute   Adulterate, Befoul, Besmear, Contaminate, Corrupt, Debase, Debauch, Defile, Dirty, Dishonour, Infect, Poison, Smear, Soil, Spoil, Stain, Taint, Violate

Possess   Contain, Control, Hold, Inhabit, Obtain, Own, Seize

Postpone   Delay, Impede

Pound   Bang, Batter, Beat, Hammer, Pulverise, Slug, Squash, Wallop

Praise   Acclaim, Admire, Applaud, Bless, Commend, Compliment, Congratulate, Emblazon, Exalt, Extol, Glorify, Hail, Hallow, Honour, Idolise, Laud, Reward, Salute, Thank, Toast, Trumpet

Precede   Guide, Lead

Preoccupy   Bemuse, Engulf, Hold, Involve, Occupy

Prepare   Adapt, Arm, Brief, Coach, Equip, Groom, Warn

Press, 1   Agitate, Compel, Constrain, Dab, Force, Goad, Hasten, Impel, Implore, Importune, Persuade, Pressure, Pressurise, Push, Quicken, Rush, Urge

Press, 2   Clasp, Crush, Embrace, Hug, Squash, Squeeze

Pressure   Cajole, Force, Goad, Press, Pressurise

Pressurise   Brutalise, Bulldoze, Constrain, Enforce, Force, Impel, Lobby, Press, Pressure, Push, Stress

Prick   Cut, Impale, Needle, Penetrate, Perforate, Pierce, Puncture, Scratch, Spike, Sting

Prime   Arm, Brief, Groom, Prepare, Season

Prize   Award, Cherish, Enshrine, Honour, Revere, Treasure, Value, Venerate

Probe   Cross-examine, Dissect, Interrogate, Investigate, Penetrate, Poke, Prod, Pump, Query, Question, Scrutinise, Search, Test

Process   Absorb, Digest

Proclaim   Glorify, Emblazon, Extol, Trumpet

Procure   Attain, Enlist, Recruit

Prod, 1   Dig, Elbow, Goad, Jab, Nudge, Poke, Probe, Push, Remind, Shove, Sting

Prod, 2   Arouse, Encourage, Goad, Impel, Incite, Motivate, Needle, Persuade, Shove, Spur, Stimulate, Urge

Profane   Curse, Desecrate, Violate

Prohibit   Ban, Bar, Block, Boycott, Censor, Debar, Deter, Disallow, Disqualify, Discourage, Exclude, Forbid, Indict, Inhibit, Interdict, Negate, Obstruct, Ostracise, Outlaw, Restrain, Restrict, Stop

Programme   Control

Promote   Abet, Aggrandise, Assist, Back, Boost, Champion, Commend, Elevate, Encourage, Exalt, Favour, Forward, Further, Help, Invigorate, Patronise, Provoke, Push, Raise, Spur, Support, Upgrade

P

Prompt   Activate, Advise, Cue, Generate,
    Goad, Impel, Instigate, Remind, Spur,
    Stimulate, Trigger

Propel   Drive, Expel, Fling, Goad, Impel,
    Incite, Inspire, Launch, Move, Push,
    Slam, Sling, Stimulate, Throw, Thrust

Propitiate   Appease, Conciliate, Mollify,
    Pacify, Placate, Reconcile, Soothe

Prosecute   Accuse, Charge, Enforce, Indict

Prostitute   Auction, Hawk, Pimp, Sell

Prostrate   Conquer, Overcome

Protect   Arm, Barricade, Chaperone, Cushion,
    Defend, Fortify, Guard, Harbour,
    Inoculate, Insulate, Insure, Patronise,
    Safeguard, Screen, Secure, Shield,
    Strengthen, Support, Wrap

Provoke, 1   Abet, Affront, Aggravate, Annoy,
    Antagonise, Bait, Beget, Dare, Defy, Enrage,
    Exasperate, Fan, Fire, Fret, Galvanise,
    Generate, Harass, Hector, Incite, Infuriate,
    Instigate, Irk, Irritate, Madden, Motivate,
    Nag, Needle, Promote, Quicken, Taunt,
    Torment, Trigger, Waken, Vex

Provoke, 2   Arouse, Awaken, Enkindle,
    Excite, Inspire, Kindle, Raise, Spark,
    Spur, Stimulate, Stir, Tantalise, Tease,
    Tickle, Titillate, Vitalise

Prune   Cut

Pull   Attract, Beckon, Draw, Extract, Grab,
    Magnetise, Move, Pick, Tug, Wrench,
    Wrest, Yank

Pulverise   Beat, Break, Bruise, Crush, Demolish,
    Mince, Pound, Shatter, Smash, Thrash

Pummel   Bang, Batter, Beat, Hammer, Pelt,
    Thump, Wallop

Pump   Cross-examine, Interrogate, Probe,
    Question, Quiz

Punch   Assault, Bash, Bat, Beat, Flog,
    Hammer, Hit, Jab, Knock, Slug, Smack,
    Strike, Thump, Wallop

Puncture   Deflate, Impale, Perforate, Pierce, Prick, Stab

Punish   Afflict, Avenge, Castigate, Chastise, Condemn, Demote, Discipline, Reprove, Torture

Purge   Absolve, Exonerate, Purify

Purify   Absolve, Cleanse, Exonerate, Purge, Redeem, Refine, Sanctify, Sanitise

Purloin   Appropriate, Filch, Nick, Pilfer, Pinch, Rob, Steal, Swipe

Pursue   Chase, Court, Desire, Entice, Follow, Harry, Hound, Hunt, Mob, Persecute, Romance, Stalk, Study, Track, Woo

Push, 1   Bump, Crowd, Drive, Elbow, Force, Hurry, Hustle, Jostle, Knock, Nudge, Poke, Press, Pressurise, Prod, Propel, Quicken, Shoulder, Shove, Spur, Thrust

Push, 2   Champion, Forward, Further, Goad, Hasten, Impel, Motivate, Patronise, Promote, Urge

Puzzle   Baffle, Bamboozle, Befuddle, Bewilder, Confound, Confuse, Daze, Derange, Distract, Dumbfound, Elude, Faze, Floor, Flummox, Foil, Mystify, Perplex, Stump

P

Qualify   Authorise, Certify, Enable, Entitle,
        License, Permit
Quash   Beat, Crush, Defeat, Demolish,
        Destroy, Overpower, Overwhelm, Quell,
        Repress, Squash, Suppress, Vanquish
Quell   Calm, Conquer, Deaden, Defeat,
        Demolish, Destroy, Lull, Mollify,
        Overpower, Pacify, Quash, Quieten,
        Repress, Silence, Soothe, Stifle, Subdue,
        Subjugate, Suppress, Vanquish
Query   Probe, Question
Question   Catechise, Challenge, Contest,
        Cross-examine, Grill, Interrogate,
        Interview, Investigate, Probe, Pump,
        Query, Quiz
Quicken   Accelerate, Electrify, Energise,
        Enliven, Excite, Exhilarate, Fire,
        Galvanise, Generate, Goad, Hasten,
        Hurry, Incite, Instigate, Invigorate,
        Motivate, Press, Provoke, Push, Rouse,
        Rush, Stimulate, Urge, Vitalise
Quieten   Allay, Alleviate, Appease, Assuage,
        Calm, Comfort, Curb, Deaden,
        Disburden, Dull, Ease, Gag, Hush, Lull,
        Mollify, Muffle, Muzzle, Pacify, Quell,
        Relax, Settle, Silence, Soothe, Stifle, Still,
        Suppress, Tranquillise

Quiz   Catechise, Cross-examine, Grill,
        Interrogate, Interview, Pump, Question,
        Test

Rag   Ridicule, Tease, Torment

Raid   Assault, Attack, Invade, Ransack, Seize

Raise, 1   Cultivate, Father, Foster, Nurture, Rear

Raise, 2   Aggrandise, Animate, Boost, Brighten, Elate, Elevate, Ennoble, Exalt, Excite, Exhilarate, Generate, Hearten, Heighten, Hoist, Inspirit, Lift, Promote, Reinforce, Strengthen, Swell, Uphold, Uplift, Upraise

Raise, 3   Conjure, Summon

Rally, 1   Animate, Cheer, Embolden, Encourage, Enthuse, Exhort, Hearten, Incite, Inspire, Inspirit, Reassure, Rouse, Stimulate, Strengthen

Rally, 2   Assemble, Congregate, Conjoin, Reassemble, Unify, Unite

Ram   Attack, Charge, Strike, Wedge

Rank   Categorise, Class, Classify, Gauge, Grade, Rate, Value

Rankle   Aggravate

Ransack   Despoil, Fleece, Plunder, Raid, Rob, Strip

Rap   Bat, Flick, Hit, Knock, Slap, Spank, Strike, Swat, Thump

Rape   Assault, Debauch, Deflower, Despoil, Impregnate, Molest, Ravish, Violate

Rate   Class, Classify, Gauge, Grade, Rank, Value

Ratify   Affirm, Approve, Authorise, Back, Champion, Endorse, Favour, Recommend, Sanction, Support

Ration   Restrain, Restrict

Rattle   Agitate, Annoy, Disconcert, Disturb, Fluster, Irritate, Shake, Unsettle

Ravage   Demolish, Despoil, Destroy, Devastate, Invade, Penetrate, Plunder, Shatter, Wreck

R

107

Ravish, 1   Debauch, Deflower, Rape, Violate,
Wreck

Ravish, 2   Captivate, Charm, Enchant,
Enrapture, Entrance, Transport

Raze   Annihilate, Bulldoze, Cancel, Cut,
Demolish, Destroy, Devastate, Efface,
Eradicate, Flatten, Obliterate

Reach   Access, Attain

Read   Compute, Examine, Scan, Study

Rear   Cultivate, Develop, Father, Foster,
Nurture, Raise

Reassemble, 1   Mend, Rebuild, Reconstruct,
Repair, Restore

Reassemble, 2   Rally

Reassure   Assure, Bolster, Cheer, Comfort,
Console, Embolden, Encourage, Fortify,
Hearten, Inspirit, Invigorate, Nerve,
Rally, Settle, Stimulate, Strengthen,
Sustain

Rebuff   Chide, Condemn, Defeat, Deflect,
Discourage, Knock, Neglect, Oppose,
Reject, Repel, Reprimand, Resist,
Sidestep, Snub, Spurn

Rebuild   Reassemble, Reconstruct, Restore

Rebuke   Abuse, Admonish, Berate, Castigate,
Censure, Chastise, Chide, Disclaim,
Lambast, Reprehend, Reprimand,
Reproach, Reprove, Scold

Recapture   Retrieve, Reclaim, Regain

Receive   Accept, Acknowledge, Admit, Adopt,
Embrace, Greet, Welcome

Reclaim   Appropriate, Recapture, Regain,
Restore, Retrieve, Salvage

Recognise   Acknowledge, Admit, Apprehend,
Greet, Salute

Recommend   Affirm, Aver, Back, Commend,
Confirm, Endorse, Favour, Ratify,
Sanction, Support, Sustain, Warrant

Recompense   Compensate, Pay, Remunerate,
Reward

Reconcile (PL)   Appease, Content, Harmonise,
        Heal, Pacify, Placate, Propitiate
Recondition   Repair, Restore
Reconstitute   Reconstruct, Restore
Reconstruct   Reassemble, Rebuild, Recapture,
        Reconstitute, Reform, Regain, Rehabilitate,
        Renew, Restore, Revolutionise, Salvage
Recruit   Employ, Engage, Enlist, Procure
Redeem, 1   Rescue, Restore
Redeem, 2   Absolve, Deliver, Discharge,
        Disentangle, Free, Liberate, Purify,
        Rescue, Restore, Save, Unburden, Untie
Redirect   Deflect, Divert
Reduce, 1   Break, Deaden, Debase, Debilitate,
        Degrade, Demote, Deplete, Deprive,
        Devalue, Diminish, Disable, Drain,
        Enervate, Exhaust, Humble, Impoverish,
        Lessen, Salvage, Sap, Starve, Subjugate,
        Subordinate, Vanquish, Weaken
Reduce, 2   Lessen, Lower
Referee   Adjudicate, Arbitrate, Judge, Umpire
Refine   Civilise, Complete, Cultivate,
        Develop, Educate, Elevate, Improve,
        Perfect, Polish, Purify
Reflect   Ape, Copy, Mirror
Reform   Alter, Amend, Better, Change, Correct,
        Improve, Modify, Reconstruct, Regenerate,
        Rehabilitate, Repair, Restore, Transform
Refresh   Aid, Cheer, Energise, Enliven,
        Exhilarate, Freshen, Invigorate,
        Regenerate, Reinvigorate, Rejuvenate,
        Revitalise, Revive, Stimulate, Titivate

R

Refuse   Debar, Decline, Deny, Exclude, Reject,
        Repel, Repudiate, Spurn
Regain   Recapture, Reclaim, Retrieve
Regale   Amuse, Divert, Entertain, Indulge
Regenerate   Cure, Energise, Heal, Inspirit,
        Invigorate, Mend, Reform, Refresh,
        Rejuvenate, Remedy, Restore, Revive,
        Stimulate, Uplift

Regulate   Balance, Ground, Moderate,
        Normalise, Order, Police, Regularise,
        Settle, Stabilise
Regularise   Demobilise, Normalise, Regulate
Rehabilitate   Reconstruct, Reform, Reinvigorate,
        Renew, Renovate, Restitute, Restore
Reinforce   Augment, Boost, Bolster, Brace, Fortify,
        Harden, Improve, Inure, Raise, Replenish,
        Secure, Strengthen, Support, Toughen
Reinvigorate   Refresh, Rehabilitate,
        Strengthen
Reject   Abandon, Banish, Betray, Boycott,
        Defy, Desert, Discard, Disclaim, Disown,
        Disregard, Ditch, Divorce, Drop, Dump,
        Eject, Eliminate, Exclude, Expel, Ignore,
        Jilt, Rebuff, Refuse, Renounce,
        Repudiate, Scorn, Spurn
Rejuvenate   Refresh, Regenerate, Invigorate,
        Strengthen
Rekindle   Kindle, Revive
Relax   Allay, Alleviate, Appease, Assuage,
        Calm, Comfort, Disburden, Ease, Lighten,
        Massage, Mollify, Pacify, Quieten, Relieve,
        Settle, Soothe, Tranquillise
Release   Absolve, Acquit, Deliver, Discharge,
        Disencumber, Disengage, Disentangle,
        Disenthrall, Emancipate, Enfranchise,
        Exonerate, Free, Liberate, Relieve,
        Rescue, Unbridle, Unburden, Unchain,
        Undo, Undo, Unfasten, Unfetter,
        Unhook, Unshackle, Untie
Relieve   Aid, Allay, Alleviate, Appease, Assist,
        Assuage, Clear, Comfort, Console, Cure,
        Cushion, Disburden, Disencumber, Dis-
        entangle, Ease, Free, Help, Lighten, Lull,
        Pacify, Relax, Release, Rescue, Settle, Spare,
        Succour, Unburden, Unfasten, Untie
Relinquish   Abandon, Desert, Discard,
        Forsake, Jilt, Leave, Renounce,
        Surrender, Yield

Relish   Savour

Remedy   Aid, Alleviate, Cure, Heal, Help,
     Improve, Mend, Regenerate, Treat

Remind   Nudge, Prod, Prompt

Remodel   Adapt, Alter

Remove   Dislodge, Dismiss, Eject, Eradicate,
     Evacuate, Excise, Exterminate, Fire

Renew   Reconstruct, Rehabilitate, Renovate,
     Restitute, Restore, Replenish

Renounce   Abandon, Abjure, Discard,
     Disclaim, Forsake, Leave, Nullify, Reject,
     Relinquish, Repudiate, Revoke, Sacrifice,
     Spurn, Surrender

Renovate   Rehabilitate, Renew, Restore, Revive

Renumerate   Pay, Recompense, Reward

Repair   Fix, Heal, Mend, Overhaul,
     Reassemble, Recondition, Reform, Restore

Repel   Antagonise, Deflect, Disgust, Horrify,
     Nauseate, Offend, Rebuff, Refuse,
     Repulse, Resist, Sicken

Replenish   Cure, Fill, Reinforce, Renew,
     Restore, Satiate, Saturate, Stuff

Reprehend   Berate, Blame, Castigate, Chastise,
     Chide, Rebuke, Reprove

Repress   Bully, Confine, Conquer, Crush,
     Curb, Discourage, Dishearten, Dominate,
     Gag, Intimidate, Master, Muffle, Oppress,
     Overcome, Overpower, Quash, Quell,
     Restrain, Silence, Smother, Squash, Stifle,
     Stop, Still, Stultify, Strangle, Subdue,
     Subjugate, Suppress, Tyrannise

Reprimand   Admonish, Berate, Castigate,
     Censure, Chide, Correct, Lambast,
     Lecture, Rebuff, Rebuke, Reproach, Scold

Reproach   Admonish, Berate, Blame,
     Castigate, Chide, Disparage, Rebuke,
     Reprimand, Scold

Reprove   Admonish, Castigate, Caution,
     Censure, Chide, Condemn, Correct,
     Lecture, Punish, Rebuke, Reprehend, Scold

R

Repudiate Disown, Disregard, Refuse, Reject, Renounce, Spurn, Surrender

Repulse Disgust, Nauseate, Offend, Repel, Sicken

Requisition Appropriate

Rescue Deliver, Disencumber, Disenthrall, Emancipate, Free, Liberate, Redeem, Release, Relieve, Salvage, Save, Unburden

Resist Challenge, Confront, Contradict, Obstruct, Parry, Rebuff, Repel

Respect Admire, Esteem, Honour, Revere, Value, Venerate

Restitute Compensate, Rehabilitate, Renew, Restore

Restore Aid, Alleviate, Assist, Cure, Enliven, Freshen, Heal, Help, Mend, Overhaul, Rebuild, Reclaim, Recondition, Reconstruct, Reconstitute, Redeem, Reform, Regenerate, Rehabilitate, Renew, Renovate, Repair, Replenish, Restitute, Revitalise, Revive, Salvage, Strengthen

Restrain Arrest, Bind, Block, Categorise, Censor, Chain, Confine, Constrain, Control, Cramp, Curb, Delay, Encumber, Fetter, Gag, Halt, Hamper, Hinder, Inhibit, Impede, Impound, Imprison, Incarcerate, Police, Prohibit, Ration, Repress, Restrict, Stifle, Stop, Subdue, Suppress, Tie, Tighten, Trammel

Restrict Ban, Bar, Bind, Block, Categorise, Chain, Confine, Constrain, Constrict, Cramp, Curb, Debilitate, Detain, Disable, Encumber, Enervate, Enfeeble, Fetter, Hamper, Handicap, Hinder, Impede, Impound, Incapacitate, Incarcerate, Interdict, Limit, Prohibit, Ration, Restrain, Suppress, Tie, Trammel, Weaken

Resuscitate Revitalise, Revive

Retain, 1 Employ, Engage, Enlist, Occupy

Retain, 2 Conserve, Detain, Hold, Save

112

Retard Clog, Encumber, Hamper, Handicap, Hinder, Impair, Impede, Inconvenience, Obstruct, Overload, Saddle, Trammel

Retrieve Recapture, Reclaim, Regain

Revere Admire, Adore, Adulate, Beatify, Deify, Dignify, Esteem, Glorify, Honour, Idolise, Laud, Prize, Respect, Treasure, Venerate, Worship

Revile Abuse, Denounce, Vilify

Revitalise Exhilarate, Freshen, Hearten, Refresh, Restore, Resuscitate, Revive, Titivate

Revive Aid, Animate, Arouse, Awaken, Charge, Cheer, Comfort, Encourage, Enliven, Freshen, Generate, Hearten, Inspirit, Invigorate, Lift, Refresh, Regenerate, Rekindle, Renovate, Restore, Resuscitate, Revitalise, Rouse, Titivate

Revoke Invalidate, Overrule, Renounce

Revolutionise Overturn, Reconstruct, Transform

Reward Award, Boost, Compensate, Crown, Enrich, Favour, Honour, Indulge, Pay, Praise, Recompense, Remunerate, Thank

Ridicule Deride, Heckle, Humiliate, Jeer, Jibe, Kid, Mock, Rag, Scorn, Shame, Taunt, Tease

Rile Aggravate, Annoy, Fret, Infuriate, Irk, Irritate, Nark, Needle, Vex

Rinse Bathe, Cleanse

Rip Cut, Lacerate, Slash, Slit, Split, Tear

Rival Challenge

Rivet Attract, Captivate, Engross, Enthrall, Fascinate, Hypnotise, Intrigue, Magnetise

Rob Cheat, Defraud, Deprive, Despoil, Filch, Fleece, Mug, Pilfer, Pillage, Pinch, Plunder, Purloin, Ransack, Sack, Steal, Swindle

Rock, 1 Disturb, Undermine, Wobble

Rock, 2 Calm, Comfort, Cradle

R

Romance   Court, Pursue, Seduce, Woo

Root   Anchor, Embed, Ground, Plant, Stabilise, Steady

Rouse   Activate, Agitate, Animate, Arouse, Awaken, Bestir, Boost, Brighten, Cheer, Elate, Electrify, Elevate, Embolden, Encourage, Energise, Enliven, Evoke, Excite, Exhilarate, Fan, Fire, Freshen, Galvanise, Generate, Hearten, Impassion, Impel, Incite, Inflame, Infuriate, Inspire, Inspirit, Invigorate, Jolt, Nerve, Persuade, Provoke, Quicken, Rally, Revive, Shock, Spark, Stimulate, Stir, Strengthen, Thrill, Titivate, Uplift, Vitalise, Waken

Rout   Cripple, Crush, Demolish, Destroy, Devastate, Finish, Ruin, Shatter

Rub   Buff, Caress, Massage, Scour, Stroke

Ruffle   Agitate, Annoy, Discomfit, Discomfort, Disturb, Dizzy, Fluster, Fret, Hassle, Irk, Nag, Needle, Nettle, Perturb, Shake, Unsettle, Vex

Ruin   Abuse, Batter, Cripple, Crush, Damage, Deform, Demolish, Destroy, Devastate, Finish, Impair, Impoverish, Injure, Rout, Shatter, Spoil, Wreck

Rule   Command, Conduct, Conquer, Direct, Dominate, Domineer, Govern, Guide, Master, Police, Subjugate, Tyrannise

Rumble   Expose, Shatter, Strip, Unmask, Unveil

Rush   Goad, Hasten, Hurry, Hustle, Press, Quicken, Urge

Sabotage   Cripple, Damage, Disable, Disrupt,
         Incapacitate, Undercut, Undermine

Sack, 1   Banish, Depose, Discard, Discharge,
         Dislodge, Dismiss, Dispossess, Eject,
         Fire, Oust, Suspend

Sack, 2   Devastate, Pillage, Plunder

Sacrifice   Kill, Renounce, Surrender

Sadden   Depress, Dishearten, Dismay,
         Dispirit, Distress

Saddle   Burden, Encumber, Hamper,
         Handicap, Hinder, Impede,
         Inconvenience, Oppress, Overload,
         Retard, Trammel, Trouble

Safeguard   Chaperone, Defend, Escort,
         Guard, Inoculate, Insulate, House,
         Insure, Police, Protect, Sanction, Secure,
         Shelter, Shield, Support

Salute   Exalt, Greet, Hail, Honour, Knight,
         Praise, Recognise, Signal, Trumpet

Salvage   Reclaim, Redeem, Rescue, Restore,
         Save

Sanctify   Anoint, Beatify, Bless, Consecrate,
         Deify, Dignify, Glorify, Hallow, Idolise,
         Purify

Sanction   Affirm, Approve, Authorise,
         Back, Condone, Delegate, Empower,
         Enable, Endorse, Entitle, Favour,
         License, Permit, Ratify, Recommend,
         Safeguard, Support, Warrant

Sanitise   Censor, Purify

Sap   Besiege, Debilitate, Demoralise, Deplete,
         Devitalise, Dilute, Diminish, Disable,
         Drain, Enervate, Enfeeble, Exhaust,
         Fatigue, Impair, Impoverish,
         Incapacitate, Jade, Paralyse, Reduce, Tire,
         Undermine, Unhinge, Weaken

S

Satiate   Fill, Replenish, Satisfy, Saturate, Stuff

Satirise   Caricature, Lampoon, Mock, Parody

Satisfy   Appease, Assuage, Content, Fill, Gratify, Indulge, Pacify, Placate, Please, Satiate, Suffuse

Saturate   Drench, Imbue, Infuse, Replenish, Satiate, Soak, Suffuse

Savage   Assault, Attack, Damage, Maul

Save   Aid, Assist, Liberate, Redeem, Rescue, Retain, Salvage, Spare

Savour   Relish

Scan   Compute, Examine, Read, Study

Scandalise   Disgust, Outrage, Shock

Scar   Blemish, Mar, Mark

Scare   Affright, Alarm, Frighten, Menace, Panic, Petrify, Startle, Terrify, Terrorise

School   Civilise, Coach, Cultivate, Develop, Direct, Discipline, Drill, Edify, Educate, Elevate, Enlighten, Familiarise, Guide, Improve, Indoctrinate, Inform, Instruct, Nurture, Teach, Train, Tutor

Scold   Berate, Browbeat, Castigate, Censure, Chastise, Chide, Criticise, Hector, Henpeck, Lambast, Lecture, Nag, Rebuke, Reprimand, Reproach, Reprove

Score   Cut

Scorn   Defy, Deride, Pan, Reject, Ridicule, Shame, Spurn

Scour   Rub

Scourge   Beat, Flog, Thrash, Torment, Torture, Whip

Scratch   Cut, Damage, Nick, Pick, Prick, Wound

Screen   Protect, Shelter, Shield, Shroud

Scrub   Cleanse, Wash

Scrutinise   Analyse, Dissect, Examine, Inspect, Investigate, Probe, Study, Vet

Sculpt   Mould, Shape

Search   Frisk, Inspect, Probe

Season   Acclimatise, Accustom, Familiarise, Habituate, Prime, Temper

116

Secure, 1   Affix, Anchor, Attain, Bind, Chain,
Fix, Lash, Lock, Peg, Pin, Reinforce,
Steady, Tie

Secure, 2   Assure, Barricade, Defend, Fortify,
Guard, Protect, Safeguard, Strengthen,
Support

Second   Abet, Assist, Back, Champion,
Support

Sedate   Calm, Ease, Settle, Sober, Tranquillise

Seduce   Allure, Attract, Beguile, Bribe, Court,
Delight, Ensnare, Entice, Entrap, Induce,
Lure, Romance, Tempt, Titillate, Turn,
Violate

Segregate   Isolate, Separate

Seize   Abduct, Arrest, Captivate, Clasp,
Clutch, Embrace, Grab, Grasp, Grip,
Hijack, Kidnap, Nail, Pluck, Possess,
Raid, Snare, Snatch

Select   Appoint, Choose, Designate, Elect,
Nominate, Pick

Sell   Auction, Pimp, Prostitute

Separate (PL)   Cleave, Detach, Divide,
Isolate, Segregate, Split, Sunder

Serve   Aid, Assist, Attend, Follow, Help, Obey,
Oblige

Sever   Amputate, Break, Cleave, Cut

Settle   Allay, Assure, Balance, Calm, Compose,
Ease, Ground, Harmonise, Heal, Lull, Pacify,
Quieten, Reassure, Regulate, Relax, Relieve,
Sedate, Soothe, Tranquillise

Shackle   Bind, Confine, Encumber, Enslave,
Fetter, Hold, Manacle, Pinion, Tie,
Trammel

Shake   Agitate, Beat, Jolt, Rattle, Ruffle,
Stir, Unnerve

Shame   Debase, Debauch, Defame, Defile,
Degrade, Demote, Devalue, Discomfit,
Discompose, Disgrace, Dishonour,
Embarrass, Expose, Humble, Humiliate,
Mock, Ridicule, Scorn, Taint

S

Shape   Adapt, Condition, Convert, Educate,
          Mould, Sculpt

Sharpen   Improve, Strengthen, Vitalise

Shatter   Batter, Blast, Break, Burst, Crack,
            Crumble, Crush, Dash, Demolish,
            Destroy, Devastate, Disunite, Fragment,
            Plunder, Pulverise, Ravage, Rout, Ruin,
            Smash, Splinter, Split, Wreck

Shelter   Accommodate, Defend, Guard,
            House, Safeguard, Screen, Shield

Shepherd   Chaperone, Conduct, Control,
             Guide, Lead, Steer

Shield   Cover, Cushion, Defend, Guard,
           Harbour, House, Protect, Safeguard,
           Screen, Shelter

Shirk   Avoid, Dodge, Elude, Escape, Evade,
          Hedge

Shock   Affright, Agitate, Amaze, Animate,
          Appal, Astonish, Astound, Bewilder,
          Bump, Daze, Disgust, Disturb, Electrify,
          Excite, Fire, Flabbergast, Frighten,
          Galvanise, Horrify, Invigorate, Jolt,
          Outrage, Rouse, Scandalise, Startle,
          Stimulate, Stir, Stun, Terrify, Thrill,
          Traumatise, Unsettle

Shoot   Execute, Fire, Launch

Shoulder   Bear, Bump, Carry, Hold, Nudge,
             Push, Support

Shove   Bump, Crowd, Elbow, Hustle, Jostle,
          Knock, Nudge, Poke, Prod, Push

Shroud   Dim, Eclipse, Enclose, Enfold,
           Envelop, Enwrap, Obscure, Overshadow,
           Screen, Swathe, Veil, Wrap

Shun   Abandon, Avoid, Desert, Dodge, Elude,
         Escape, Evade, Ostracise

Sicken   Appal, Disgust, Disown, Horrify,
           Nauseate, Offend, Repel, Repulse, Weary

Sidestep   Avoid, Dodge, Elude, Evade,
             Outrun, Rebuff

Signal   Alarm, Alert, Beckon, Salute

Silence   Calm, Curb, Gag, Hush, Lull, Muffle,
Mute, Muzzle, Quell, Quieten, Repress,
Stifle, Still, Stop, Subdue, Suppress, Throttle

Sink   Drown, Swamp

Skewer   Impale, Knife, Pierce, Spike, Stab

Skin   Bamboozle, Expose, Flay, Fleece, Peel,
Uncover

Slam   Bang, Bash, Propel, Slap, Strike,
Thrash, Thump

Slander   Abuse, Affront, Attack, Blacken,
Defame, Discredit, Disparage, Impugn,
Insult, Knock, Malign, Outrage, Slight,
Taunt

Slap   Bang, Beat, Clobber, Flog, Hit, Rap,
Slam, Slug, Smack, Smite, Sock, Strike,
Wallop, Whack

Slash   Chop, Cleave, Cut, Gash, Gouge,
Hack, Incise, Knife, Lacerate, Rip, Slit,
Strike, Tear

Slaughter   Annihilate, Butcher, Crush,
Destroy, Exterminate, Massacre, Murder

Slay   Annihilate, Butcher, Eliminate, Execute,
Kill, Liquidate, Murder, Terminate

Slight   Affront, Insult, Mock, Offend, Slander,
Snub

Sling   Chuck, Fling, Propel, Throw

Slit   Cleave, Cut, Gash, Gouge, Incise, Knife,
Lacerate, Pierce, Rip, Slash, Split, Tear,
Wound

Slug   Bat, Batter, Beat, Belt, Clobber, Hit,
Knock, Pound, Punch, Slap, Sock,
Spank, Thump, Wallop, Whack

Smack   Bang, Bat, Beat, Clip, Clobber, Clout,
Cuff, Flog, Hit, Punch, Slap, Spank,
Strike, Swat, Swipe, Thump, Whack

Smash   Batter, Break, Crush, Dash, Demolish,
Destroy, Devastate, Pulverise, Shatter

Smear   Besmear, Blacken, Contaminate,
Defile, Dirty, Foul, Pollute, Soil, Stain,
Taint

S

119

Smite   Batter, Belt, Cleave, Flog, Hit, Slap, Sock, Swat, Wallop, Whack

Smooth   Calm, Ease, Humour, Level, Soothe, Tranquillise

Smother   Choke, Coddle, Cosset, Deaden, Extinguish, Muffle, Repress, Strangle, Stifle, Suffocate, Suppress, Stifle, Strangle, Swathe

Snap   Break, Crack, Flip

Snare   Capture, Catch, Embroil, Enmesh, Ensnare, Entangle, Entrap, Hook, Implicate, Seize, Trammel, Trap

Snatch   Abduct, Capture, Catch, Clutch, Grab, Hijack, Nab, Pluck, Seize

Snub   Abandon, Humble, Humiliate, Ignore, Insult, Offend, Ostracise, Overlook, Rebuff, Slight

Soak   Douse, Drench, Infuse, Saturate

Sober   Awaken, Calm, Compose, Cool, Depress, Sedate, Steady

Sock   Batter, Beat, Belt, Box, Clobber, Cuff, Flog, Hammer, Hit, Knock, Lambast, Slap, Slug, Smite, Spank, Strike, Wallop, Whack

Soil   Defile, Dirty, Foul, Pollute, Smear, Stain, Taint

Solicit   Beg, Beseech, Entreat, Implore, Importune

Soothe   Allay, Alleviate, Appease, Assuage, Calm, Comfort, Compose, Conciliate, Console, Disburden, Ease, Harmonise, Heal, Hush, Lighten, Lull, Mollify, Pacify, Placate, Propitiate, Quell, Quieten, Relax, Settle, Smooth, Stroke, Sweeten, Temper, Tranquillise

Sophisticate   Better, Civilise, Groom, Mature

Sour   Alienate, Disaffect, Disenchant, Disillusion, Embitter, Envenom, Poison

Spank   Bang, Beat, Flagellate, Hammer, Rap, Slug, Smack, Sock, Strap, Strike, Tan, Thrash, Thwack, Wallop, Whack, Whip

Spare   Exempt, Excuse, Relieve, Save

Spark   Animate, Arouse, Excite, Generate, Ignite, Incite, Inspire, Kindle, Provoke, Rouse, Stimulate, Stir, Trigger

Spellbind   Beguile, Bewitch, Captivate, Charm, Delight, Enamour, Enchant, Engross, Enrapture, Enthrall, Entrance, Grip, Hypnotise, Mesmerise, Transfix

Spike   Impale, Pierce, Prick, Skewer, Stab

Splinter   Break, Crack, Crumble, Disunite, Fracture, Fragment, Shatter, Split

Split, 1   Break, Burst, Crack, Crumble, Cut, Fracture, Fragment, Gouge, Incise, Rip, Shatter, Slit, Splinter, Tear

Split, 2 (PL)   Bisect, Cleave, Disunite, Divide, Sunder, Separate

Spoil, 1   Contaminate, Damage, Deform, Impair, Injure, Mar, Pollute, Ruin, Taint

Spoil, 2   Favour, Indulge, Mollycoddle, Pamper, Pet

Sponsor   Back, Support

Spook   Frighten, Terrify

Spur   Accelerate, Animate, Arouse, Assist, Awaken, Boost, Drive, Encourage, Energise, Forward, Further, Galvanise, Generate, Goad, Impel, Incite, Inspire, Motivate, Prod, Promote, Prompt, Provoke, Push, Stimulate, Strengthen, Support, Uphold, Urge, Vitalise

Spurn   Banish, Desert, Discard, Disclaim, Disregard, Drop, Eject, Exclude, Expel, Ignore, Rebuff, Refuse, Reject, Renounce, Repudiate, Scorn

Squash   Bulldoze, Crush, Flatten, Mash, Pound, Press, Quash, Repress, Squeeze, Suppress, Trample

Squeeze   Clasp, Clinch, Cuddle, Embrace, Hug, Oppress, Pinch, Press, Squash

Stab   Impale, Knife, Penetrate, Perforate, Pierce, Puncture, Skewer, Spike, Wound

S

121

Stabilise   Anchor, Assure, Balance, Normalise,
        Regulate, Root, Steady, Support

Stagger   Amaze, Astonish, Astound, Daze,
        Dumbfound, Flabbergast, Stun, Surprise

Stain   Besmear, Blacken, Contaminate, Defile,
        Dirty, Foul, Pollute, Smear, Soil, Taint

Stalk   Chase, Follow, Hunt, Pursue

Stall   Divert, Evade, Halt, Parry, Stop

Startle   Agitate, Alarm, Amaze, Astonish,
        Confound, Daze, Electrify, Excite,
        Frighten, Galvanise, Jolt, Scare, Shock,
        Stimulate, Stir, Surprise, Thrill

Starve   Reduce, Weaken

Steady   Balance, Ground, Level, Root, Secure,
        Sober, Stabilise, Support

Steal   Appropriate, Despoil, Filch, Hijack,
        Nick, Pilfer, Pinch, Purloin, Rob, Swipe

Steel   Harden, Stiffen, Toughen

Steer   Direct, Dominate, Govern, Guide,
        Influence, Lead, Manage, Manipulate,
        Manoeuvre, Navigate, Operate,
        Shepherd, Usher

Stiffen   Embolden, Harden, Invigorate, Steel

Stifle   Choke, Curb, Cushion, Deaden, Gag,
        Hush, Muffle, Mute, Muzzle, Quell, Quieten,
        Repress, Restrain, Silence, Smother, Still,
        Stop, Strangle, Subdue, Suppress, Throttle

Still   Allay, Alleviate, Appease, Assuage, Calm,
        Curb, Disburden, Quieten, Repress,
        Silence, Suppress, Stifle

Stimulate   Accelerate, Activate, Agitate,
        Amaze, Animate, Arouse, Astonish,
        Awaken, Boost, Brighten, Cheer, Drive,
        Electrify, Embolden, Encourage,
        Energise, Enliven, Excite, Exhilarate,
        Fan, Fire, Freshen, Galvanise, Generate,
        Goad, Hearten, Heat, Impassion, Impel,
        Incite, Inflame, Inspire, Inspirit,
        Instigate, Invigorate, Jolt, Motivate,
        Move, Nerve, Prod, Prompt, Propel,

Provoke, Quicken, Rally, Reassure,
Refresh, Regenerate, Rouse, Shock,
Spark, Spur, Startle, Stir, Stoke, Thrill,
Tickle, Titillate, Urge, Vitalise, Waken

Sting   Cut, Goad, Hurt, Needle, Prick, Prod,
Wound

Stir   Activate, Affect, Agitate, Amaze, Arouse,
Astound, Awaken, Cheer, Churn,
Disturb, Electrify, Embolden, Encourage,
Energise, Galvanise, Generate, Hearten,
Heat, Impassion, Incite, Inflame, Inspire,
Inspirit, Invigorate, Jolt, Move, Nerve,
Provoke, Rouse, Shake, Shock, Spark,
Startle, Stimulate, Stoke, Stump, Thrill,
Touch, Vitalise, Waken

Stoke   Cajole, Encourage, Excite, Fire, Fuel,
Inflame, Kindle, Stimulate, Stir, Stump

Stomach   Abide, Suffer, Tolerate

Stone   Execute, Strike

Stop   Apprehend, Arrest, Ban, Bar, Block,
Check, Constrain, Deflect, Detain,
Forestall, Halt, Hold, Immobilise,
Impede, Inactivate, Inhibit, Intercept,
Interdict, Mute, Muzzle, Obstruct,
Prohibit, Repress, Restrain, Silence, Stall,
Stifle, Thwart

Storm   Assault, Attack

Strangle   Choke, Extinguish, Muffle, Repress,
Stifle, Smother, Suffocate, Suppress, Throttle

Strap   Beat, Birch, Cane, Castigate, Flagellate,
Flog, Lash, Spank, Tan, Thrash, Tie,
Whip, Yoke

Strengthen   Abet, Aid, Arm, Assist, Augment,
Bolster, Boost, Brace, Cheer, Comfort,
Concentrate, Corroborate, Elevate,
Embolden, Encourage, Exalt, Excite,
Favour, Feed, Fire, Fortify, Forward,
Fuel, Further, Harden, Hearten,
Heighten, Help, Improve, Inflame,
Inspirit, Inure, Invigorate, Nerve,

S

Nurture, Protect, Raise, Rally, Reassure, Reinforce, Reinvigorate, Rejuvenate, Restore, Rouse, Secure, Sharpen, Spur, Succour, Support, Sustain, Swell, Toughen, Urge, Vitalise

Stress   Oppress, Pressurise

Strike   Assault, Astound, Attack, Bang, Bat, Batter, Bang, Beat, Break, Bump, Charge, Clobber, Crown, Cuff, Cut, Dash, Hammer, Hit, Lash, Pelt, Punch, Ram, Rap, Slam, Slap, Slash, Slug, Smack, Sock, Spank, Stone, Stun, Swat, Swipe, Tap, Thrash, Thump, Thwack, Wallop, Whack, Wound

Strip   Belt, Expose, Fleece, Ransack, Uncover, Undress, Unmask

Stroke   Brush, Caress, Fondle, Massage, Pat, Paw, Pet, Rub, Soothe, Touch

Study   Analyse, Compute, Dissect, Examine, Observe, Peruse, Pursue, Read, Scrutinise

Stuff   Fill, Replenish, Satiate

Stultify   Frustrate, Hamper, Impede, Numb, Obstruct, Repress, Suppress, Thwart, Wedge

Stump   Baffle, Befuddle, Bewilder, Block, Confound, Confuse, Dumbfound, Elude, Floor, Flummox, Foil, Forestall, Mystify, Outwit, Perplex, Puzzle, Stir, Stoke, Thwart

Stun   Amaze, Arrest, Astonish, Astound, Bemuse, Bewilder, Confound, Daze, Dumbfound, Flabbergast, Freeze, Immobilise, Numb, Paralyse, Petrify, Shock, Stagger, Strike, Stupefy, Surprise, Wind

Stupefy   Amaze, Astonish, Astound, Bemuse, Bewilder, Daze, Dazzle, Inebriate, Numb, Stun

Subdue   Break, Control, Curb, Crush, Humble, Hush, Master, Mellow, Oppress, Overwhelm, Pacify, Quell, Quieten, Repress, Restrain, Silence, Stifle, Subjugate, Suppress

Subjugate   Bind, Capture, Conquer, Discipline, Quell, Reduce, Repress, Rule, Subdue, Suppress, Tame

Submerge   Bury, Drown, Obliterate, Overwhelm, Suppress, Swamp

Subordinate   Devalue, Lessen, Lower, Reduce

Subsume   Contain, Cover, Encompass, Hold, Include, Incorporate

Succour   Abet, Aid, Assist, Back, Encourage, Forward, Further, Help, Nurse, Relieve, Strengthen, Support, Sustain

Suffer   Abide, Bear, Endure, Tolerate, Stomach, Weather

Suffocate   Choke, Smother, Strangle

Suffuse   Fill, Infuse, Satisfy, Saturate

Summon   Beckon, Call, Conjure, Evoke, Raise, Invoke

Sunder (PL)   Bisect, Cleave, Divide, Separate, Split

Support, 1   Abet, Affirm, Aid, Assist, Authorise, Aver, Back, Bear, Befriend, Bolster, Boost, Brace, Carry, Champion, Commend, Condone, Corroborate, Defend, Encourage, Endorse, Endure, Espouse, Favour, Fortify, Foster, Forward, Further, Help, Nourish, Nurse, Nurture, Patronise, Protect, Promote, Ratify, Recommend, Reinforce, Safeguard, Sanction, Second, Secure, Sponsor, Spur, Stabilise, Steady, Strengthen, Succour, Sustain, Upgrade, Uphold, Vindicate, Warrant

Support, 2   Bear, Carry, Cradle, Hold, Shoulder

Suppress   Arrest, Ban, Crush, Curb, Deaden, Demolish, Discourage, Extinguish, Gag, Hush, Muffle, Muzzle, Oppress, Overmaster, Overpower, Quash, Quell, Quieten, Repress, Restrain, Restrict, Silence, Smother, Squash, Stifle, Still, Strangle, Stultify, Submerge, Subdue, Subjugate, Throttle, Tyrannise

Surmount   Overcome

Surpass   Better, Eclipse, Exceed, Outdo,
Outshine, Top, Transcend

Surrender   Abandon, Forsake, Relinquish,
Renounce, Repudiate, Sacrifice, Yield

Surprise   Amaze, Ambush, Astonish,
Astound, Bewilder, Confound, Daze,
Flabbergast, Stagger, Startle, Stun

Surround   Besiege, Circle, Circumscribe,
Contain, Encircle, Enclose, Encompass,
Enfold, Envelop, Hug, Wrap

Suspend, 1   Dangle

Suspend, 2   Depose, Sack

Sustain   Assist, Augment, Back, Bear, Bolster,
Cheer, Comfort, Embolden, Encourage,
Endorse, Feed, Fortify, Foster, Fuel,
Hearten, Invigorate, Nourish, Nurture,
Reassure, Recommend, Strengthen,
Succour, Support, Wean

Swamp   Besiege, Consume, Deluge, Engulf,
Envelop, Infest, Inundate, Overwhelm,
Sink, Submerge

Swat   Bat, Hit, Rap, Smack, Smite, Strike,
Swipe

Swathe   Clasp, Embrace, Enclose, Enfold,
Envelop, Enwrap, Shroud, Smother,
Wrap

Sweeten   Alleviate, Appease, Mollify, Pacify,
Soothe, Thaw

Swell   Aggrandise, Augment, Boost, Distend,
Elevate, Exalt, Fill, Heighten, Inflate,
Lift, Raise, Strengthen

Swindle   Bamboozle, Cheat, Con, Deceive,
Defraud, Delude, Diddle, Dupe, Exploit,
Gull, Hoodwink, Fiddle, Fleece, Hoax,
Rob, Trick

Swipe, 1   Beat, Smack, Strike, Swat, Wound

Swipe, 2   Filch, Nick, Pinch, Purloin, Steal

Tackle   Attack, Broach, Challenge, Confront

Tag   Classify

Taint   Adulterate, Besmear, Blacken, Blemish,
Blight, Contaminate, Corrupt, Damage,
Debase, Defile, Dirty, Disgrace,
Dishonour, Foul, Impair, Infect, Mar,
Poison, Pollute, Shame, Smear, Soil,
Spoil, Stain

Tame   Discipline, Subjugate, Temper

Tan   Beat, Birch, Cane, Castigate, Flagellate,
Flog, Lash, Laud, Spank, Strap, Thrash,
Whip

Tantalise   Fascinate, Provoke, Taunt, Tease,
Titillate

Tap   Dab, Flick, Pat, Strike, Touch

Tarnish   Blacken, Defame, Jibe, Mar

Taunt   Badger, Bait, Harass, Heckle, Insult, Jeer,
Jibe, Mock, Needle, Pester, Poke, Provoke,
Ridicule, Slander, Tantalise, Tease, Torment

Teach   Advise, Aid, Apprise, Civilise, Coach,
Condition, Counsel, Cultivate, Develop,
Direct, Discipline, Drill, Edify, Educate,
Elevate, Enlighten, Foster, Groom, Guide,
Improve, Indoctrinate, Inform, Instruct,
Lecture, Nurture, School, Train, Tutor

Tear   Bite, Break, Cleave, Cut, Gash, Gouge,
Incise, Lacerate, Rip, Slash, Slit, Split

Tease   Aggravate, Badger, Bait, Bother, Fret,
Goad, Harass, Harry, Hassle, Irritate,
Kid, Mock, Needle, Pester, Poke,
Provoke, Rag, Ridicule, Tantalise,
Taunt, Tickle, Torment, Vex

Temper   Allay, Assuage, Calm, Moderate,
Mollify, Season, Soothe, Tame

Tempt   Allure, Attract, Bribe, Cajole, Coax,
Entice, Induce, Influence, Lure, Seduce

T

Terminate Annihilate, Eliminate, Execute,
Finish, Kill, Murder, Slay

Terrify Affright, Alarm, Frighten, Horrify,
Panic, Paralyse, Petrify, Scare, Shock,
Spook, Terrorise

Terrorise Affright, Alarm, Blackmail, Bully,
Endanger, Frighten, Hijack, Horrify,
Intimidate, Jeopardise, Menace, Oppress,
Petrify, Plague, Scare, Terrify, Threaten

Test Appraise, Assess, Audition, Examine,
Probe, Quiz

Thank Bless, Credit, Praise, Reward

Thaw Disarm, Sweeten, Warm

Thrash Batter, Beat, Bludgeon, Defeat,
Flagellate, Flog, Pelt, Pulverise, Scourge,
Slam, Spank, Strap, Strike, Tan, Thump,
Thwack, Whip

Threaten Alarm, Blackmail, Bully, Challenge,
Curse, Compromise, Endanger, Hector,
Hijack, Imperil, Intimidate, Jeopardise,
Menace, Terrorise, Undermine, Warn

Thrill Animate, Arouse, Delight, Electrify,
Enrapture, Excite, Exhilarate, Fire,
Galvanise, Rouse, Shock, Startle,
Stimulate, Stir, Titillate

Throttle Choke, Curb, Gag, Silence, Stifle,
Strangle, Suppress

Throw Chuck, Fling, Flip, Floor, Distract,
Pelt, Propel, Sling, Toss

Thrust Drive, Further, Hustle, Propel, Push

Thump Bang, Bat, Batter, Beat, Hammer,
Hit, Pummel, Punch, Rap, Slam, Slug,
Smack, Strike, Thrash, Thwack, Wallop,
Whack

Thwack Bang, Batter, Beat, Spank, Strike,
Thrash, Thump, Whack

Thwart Block, Defeat, Defy, Delay, Elude,
Flummox, Forestall, Hamper, Hinder,
Impede, Obstruct, Outwit, Parry, Stop,
Stultify, Stump, Undo

Tickle   Amuse, Cheer, Provoke, Stimulate,
Tease, Titillate

Tie   Bind, Chain, Constrain, Encumber,
Entwine, Fetter, Fix, Hamper, Lash,
Lock, Pinion, Restrain, Restrict, Secure,
Shackle, Strap

Tighten   Constrict, Restrain

Tire   Debilitate, Devitalise, Drain, Enervate,
Enfeeble, Exhaust, Fatigue, Harass,
Incapacitate, Jade, Sap, Unnerve,
Weaken, Weary

Titillate   Arouse, Attract, Captivate, Charm,
Excite, Provoke, Seduce, Stimulate,
Tantalise, Thrill, Tickle

Titivate   Enliven, Freshen, Refresh, Revitalise,
Revive, Rouse

Toast   Glorify, Honour, Praise, Trumpet,
Warm

Tolerate   Abide, Bear, Endure, Indulge,
Stomach, Suffer

Top   Better, Outdo, Outshine, Outsmart,
Outwit, Surpass, Transcend, Trump

Topple   Depose, Dethrone, Overthrow

Torment   Aggravate, Assail, Badger, Bait,
Browbeat, Bug, Bully, Curse, Frustrate,
Harangue, Harass, Harry, Hassle, Hector,
Henpeck, Intimidate, Irritate, Maltreat, Nag,
Persecute, Pester, Plague, Provoke, Rag,
Scourge, Taunt, Tease, Torture, Trouble, Vex

Torture   Abuse, Persecute, Punish, Scourge,
Torment, Trouble

Toss   Flick, Fling, Flip, Throw

Touch, 1   Brush, Caress, Dab, Feel, Flick,
Jab, Kiss, Manipulate, Massage, Nurture,
Paw, Pat, Peck, Stir, Stroke, Tap

Touch, 2   Impress, Move

Toughen   Boost, Fortify, Harden, Reinforce,
Steel, Strengthen

Track   Accompany, Chase, Follow, Hunt,
Pursue, Stalk

T

Train   Civilise, Coach, Condition, Cultivate,
    Develop, Discipline, Drill, Edify, Educate,
    Enlighten, Familiarise, Groom, Guide,
    Improve, Indoctrinate, Inform, Instruct,
    Nurture, School, Teach, Tutor

Trammel   Burden, Confine, Constrain, Constrict,
    Cramp, Curb, Encumber, Enmesh, Ensnare,
    Entangle, Fetter, Hamper, Handicap, Hinder,
    Impede, Implicate, Inconvenience, Obstruct,
    Oppress, Overload, Restrain, Restrict,
    Retard, Saddle, Shackle, Snare, Trap

Trample   Beat, Flatten, Oppress, Squash

Tranquillise   Allay, Alleviate, Appease,
    Assuage, Calm, Deaden, Disburden, Ease,
    Lighten, Lull, Pacify, Quieten, Relax,
    Sedate, Settle, Smooth, Soothe

Transcend   Eclipse, Exceed, Outdo, Outshine,
    Surpass, Top

Transfix   Hold, Hypnotise, Mesmerise,
    Paralyse, Petrify, Spellbind

Transform   Alter, Change, Convert, Pervert,
    Reform, Revolutionise, Turn

Transport, 1   Bear, Carry, Convey

Transport, 2   Bewitch, Ravish

Trap   Ambush, Box, Catch, Corner, Enmesh,
    Ensnare, Entangle, Hoax, Hook, Implicate,
    Imprison, Net, Outsmart, Outwit,
    Pigeonhole, Snare, Trammel, Trick

Trash   Batter, Destroy, Violate

Traumatise   Shock, Trouble, Wound

Treasure   Adore, Adulate, Cherish,
    Consecrate, Conserve, Enshrine, Honour,
    Idolise, Immortalise, Pet, Prize, Revere,
    Value, Venerate, Worship

Treat, 1   Favour, Pamper

Treat, 2   Cure, Heal, Mend, Remedy

Trick   Bamboozle, Beguile, Cheat, Con, Deceive,
    Defraud, Delude, Dupe, Entrap,
    Fool, Gull, Hoax, Hoodwink, Kid,
    Manoeuvre, Mislead, Outwit, Swindle, Trap

Trigger   Activate, Cue, Fire, Generate, Ignite,
          Light, Prompt, Provoke, Spark

Trip   Outsmart, Outwit

Trouble   Afflict, Agitate, Annoy, Badger,
          Bedevil, Bother, Burden, Concern,
          Confound, Confuse, Derange,
          Discomfort, Disconcert, Distress,
          Disturb, Fret, Harass, Harm, Harry,
          Hassle, Haunt, Muddle, Perplex, Perturb,
          Pester, Plague, Saddle, Torment, Torture,
          Traumatise, Unnerve, Unsettle, Upset,
          Vex, Weaken, Weary, Worry

Trounce   Beat, Defeat, Flog, Humiliate

Trump   Outdo, Outsmart, Outwit, Top

Trumpet   Emblazon, Extol, Laud, Praise,
          Proclaim, Salute, Toast

Try   Appraise, Judge

Tug   Draw, Grab, Move, Pull, Wrench, Wrest,
          Yank

Turn   Alter, Change, Convert, Pervert,
          Seduce, Transform

Tutor   Aid, Apprise, Assist, Civilise, Coach,
          Counsel, Cultivate, Develop, Direct,
          Discipline, Drill, Edify, Educate,
          Enlighten, Groom, Guide, Help,
          Improve, Indoctrinate, Inform, Instruct,
          Lecture, School, Teach, Train

Twist   Bend, Contort, Deform, Derange,
          Deviate, Flip, Modify, Pervert, Warp,
          Wrench, Wrest, Wring

Tyrannise   Bully, Crush, Dominate, Domineer,
          Intimidate, Oppress, Persecute, Repress,
          Rule, Suppress

T

131

Umpire Adjudicate, Arbitrate, Judge,
     Mediate, Referee
Unbalance Inebriate, Intoxicate, Unhinge
Unbridle Release
Unburden Clear, Discharge, Disencumber,
     Disengage, Disentangle, Disenthrall,
     Free, Liberate, Redeem, Release, Relieve,
     Rescue, Unchain, Unfetter, Unleash,
     Unshackle
Unchain Deliver, Disencumber, Disengage,
     Disentangle, Disenthrall, Emancipate,
     Enfranchise, Free, Liberate, Release,
     Unburden, Unfetter, Unleash, Unshackle,
     Untie
Uncover, 1 Flay, Skin, Strip, Undress, Unveil
Uncover, 2 Expose, Unmask
Undercut Diminish, Disable, Enfeeble,
     Invalidate, Sabotage, Undermine,
     Weaken
Underestimate Misjudge
Undermine Compromise, Debilitate,
     Demoralise, Deplete, Devitalise, Disable,
     Diminish, Enfeeble, Rock, Sabotage, Sap,
     Threaten, Unhinge, Weaken, Wobble,
     Undercut, Unnerve
Undo, 1 Disengage, Disentangle, Free,
     Release, Unfasten
Undo, 2 Thwart
Undress Strip, Uncover
Unearth Discover
Unfasten Release, Relieve, Undo, Untie
Unfetter Disencumber, Disengage,
     Disentangle, Disenthrall, Deliver,
     Emancipate, Enfranchise, Free, Liberate,
     Release, Unburden, Unchain, Unleash,
     Unshackle, Untie

U

133

Unhinge   Confound, Confuse, Craze,
  Debilitate, Derange, Destabilise,
  Devitalise, Disable, Enfeeble, Exhaust,
  Fatigue, Inebriate, Madden, Sap,
  Unbalance, Undermine, Unsettle,
  Weaken

Unify (PL)   Conjoin, Combine, Rally, Unite
Unite (PL)   Combine, Conjoin, Rally, Unify
Unhook   Disengage, Release
Unleash   Disencumber, Disentangle,
  Disenthrall, Emancipate, Free, Liberate,
  Unburden, Unchain, Unfetter, Untie

Unmask   Expose, Rumble, Shatter, Strip,
  Uncover, Unveil

Unnerve   Agitate, Alarm, Confound, Confuse,
  Debilitate, Disarm, Disconcert, Distress,
  Enfeeble, Fluster, Incapacitate, Panic,
  Paralyse, Perturb, Shake, Tire, Trouble,
  Undermine, Unsettle, Unsteady, Upset,
  Weaken

Unravel   Decipher, Disentangle, Untie
Unsettle   Agitate, Bother, Confuse, Disconcert,
  Disturb, Dizzy, Faze, Fluster, Perturb,
  Rattle, Ruffle, Shock, Trouble, Unhinge,
  Unnerve, Unsteady, Upset, Worry

Unshackle   Deliver, Discharge, Disencumber,
  Disengage, Disentangle, Disenthrall,
  Emancipate, Enfranchise, Free, Liberate,
  Release, Unburden, Unchain, Unfetter,
  Untie

Unsteady   Derange, Destabilise, Unnerve,
  Unsettle

Untie   Discharge, Disencumber, Disengage,
  Disentangle, Disenthrall, Disunite,
  Emancipate, Free, Liberate, Redeem,
  Release, Relieve, Unchain, Unfasten,
  Unfetter, Unleash, Unravel, Unshackle

Unveil   Expose, Rumble, Shatter, Unmask
Upgrade   Aggrandise, Elevate, Forward,
  Further, Improve, Promote, Support

Uphold   Back, Befriend, Encourage, Forward, Raise, Spur, Support

Uplift   Animate, Boost, Brighten, Cheer, Elate, Elevate, Excite, Exhilarate, Freshen, Hearten, Hoist, Inspirit, Invigorate, Lift, Nurture, Raise, Regenerate, Rouse, Vitalise

Upset   Agitate, Bother, Derange, Discomfort, Discomfit, Disconcert, Disrupt, Dissatisfy, Distract, Distress, Disturb, Fluster, Fret, Harass, Madden, Nark, Offend, Perturb, Trouble, Unnerve, Unsettle, Vex

Urge   Animate, Boost, Compel, Drive, Encourage, Enforce, Entreat, Force, Forward, Goad, Hasten, Haunt, Impel, Incite, Influence, Motivate, Persuade, Press, Prod, Push, Quicken, Rush, Spur, Strengthen, Spur, Stimulate

Use, 1   Deploy, Employ, Utilise

Use, 2   Abuse, Exploit, Misuse, Use

Usher   Attend, Guide, Lead, Navigate, Steer

Utilise   Deploy, Employ, Engage, Use

U

Validate   Confirm, Permit

Value, 1   Appraise, Clasp, Class, Classify,
　　　　Grade, Rank, Rate

Value, 2   Assess, Cherish, Esteem, Enshrine,
　　　　Estimate, Honour, Prize, Respect,
　　　　Treasure

Vanquish   Beat, Conquer, Crush, Defeat,
　　　　Demolish, Destroy, Master, Overmaster,
　　　　Overpower, Overwhelm, Quash, Quell,
　　　　Reduce

Veil   Cover, Obscure, Shroud

Venerate   Admire, Adore, Adulate, Beatify,
　　　　Consecrate, Deify, Dignify, Enshrine,
　　　　Honour, Idolise, Prize, Respect, Revere,
　　　　Treasure, Worship

Vet   Appraise, Check, Dissect, Scrutinise

Vex   Aggravate, Agitate, Annoy, Badger,
　　　　Bedevil, Bug, Distress, Disturb, Fluster,
　　　　Fret, Harass, Harry, Hassle, Hound,
　　　　Incense, Infuriate, Irk, Irritate, Nag,
　　　　Nark, Nettle, Persecute, Perturb, Pester,
　　　　Plague, Provoke, Rile, Ruffle, Tease,
　　　　Torment, Trouble, Upset, Weary, Worry

Victimise   Bully, Dupe, Oppress, Persecute

Vilify   Abuse, Attack, Berate, Blacken,
　　　　Defame, Denounce, Discredit, Disparage,
　　　　Revile

Vindicate   Absolve, Acquit, Clear, Endorse,
　　　　Excuse, Exonerate, Support

Violate   Abuse, Assault, Corrupt, Debauch,
　　　　Defile, Desecrate, Pollute, Profane, Rape,
　　　　Ravish, Seduce, Trash

Vitalise   Activate, Animate, Arouse, Awaken,
　　　　Brighten, Cheer, Electrify, Embolden,
　　　　Encourage, Energise, Enliven, Excite,
　　　　Exhilarate, Fire, Galvanise, Generate,

V

137

Hearten, Inflame, Inspire, Inspirit,
Invigorate, Motivate, Nerve, Provoke,
Quicken, Rouse, Sharpen, Spur,
Stimulate, Stir, Strengthen, Uplift

Vitiate   Contaminate, Corrupt, Debase,
Poison

Vivify   Animate, Arouse, Awaken

Waken Activate, Animate, Arouse, Awaken, Enliven, Excite, Fire, Galvanise, Generate, Kindle, Provoke, Rouse, Stimulate, Stir

Wallop Bat, Batter, Beat, Belt, Clobber, Crush, Flog, Hammer, Hit, Knock, Pelt, Pound, Pummel, Punch, Slap, Slug, Smite, Sock, Spank, Strike, Thump, Whack

Warm Animate, Arouse, Cheer, Excite, Heat, Impassion, Melt, Thaw, Toast

Warn Admonish, Advise, Alarm, Alert, Caution, Counsel, Dissuade, Forewarn, Notify, Prepare, Threaten

Warp Bend, Break, Contort, Deform, Deviate, Distort, Impair, Modify, Pervert, Twist

Warrant Assure, Authorise, Back, Champion, Commission, Delegate, Endorse, Entitle, License, Permit, Recommend, Sanction, Support

Wash Cleanse, Rinse, Scrub

Weaken Adulterate, Break, Cripple, Damage, Deaden, Debase, Debilitate, Demoralise, Deplete, Depress, Deprive, Devalue, Devitalise, Dilute, Diminish, Disable, Disarm, Emasculate, Enervate, Enfeeble, Exhaust, Fatigue, Hurt, Impair, Impoverish, Incapacitate, Injure, Invalidate, Lessen, Moderate, Modify, Reduce, Restrict, Sap, Starve, Tire, Trouble, Undercut, Undermine, Unhinge, Unnerve, Wound

Wean Nourish, Nurture, Sustain

Weary Annoy, Burden, Debilitate, Drain, Exasperate, Exhaust, Fatigue, Irk, Jade, Plague, Sicken, Tire, Trouble, Vex

Weather Endure, Suffer, Withstand

W

Wed   Espouse, Marry

Wedge   Affix, Fix, Lodge, Ram, Stuff

Weigh   Consider, Contemplate, Evaluate, Examine, Gauge, Measure

Welcome   Accept, Acclaim, Adopt, Applaud, Embrace, Espouse, Greet, Hail, Invite, Receive

Whack   Bang, Batter, Beat, Belt, Box, Clobber, Cuff, Flog, Hammer, Hit, Lambast, Slap, Slug, Smack, Smite, Sock, Spank, Strike, Thump, Thwack, Wallop

Whip   Beat, Birch, Cane, Castigate, Flagellate, Flog, Lash, Scourge, Spank, Strap, Tan, Thrash

Will   Award, Encourage

Win   Allure, Attain, Attract, Captivate, Capture, Charm, Convince, Disarm, Enamour, Enchant, Persuade

Wind   Stun

Wing   Disable, Hinder, Wound

Withstand   Endure, Weather

Wobble   Disturb, Rock, Undermine

Woo   Court, Entice, Pursue, Romance

Work   Engineer, Handle, Influence, Manage, Manipulate, Operate

Worry   Agitate, Annoy, Badger, Bedevil, Bother, Concern, Distract, Distress, Disturb, Harass, Harry, Hassle, Haunt, Hector, Niggle, Persecute, Perturb, Pester, Plague, Trouble, Unease, Unsettle, Vex

Worship   Adore, Adulate, Beatify, Deify, Enshrine, Glorify, Idolise, Revere, Treasure, Venerate

Wound   Bite, Break, Bruise, Cut, Damage, Disable, Gash, Gouge, Hack, Harm, Hurt, Incise, Injure, Insult, Knife, Lacerate, Maim, Maltreat, Maul, Nick, Scratch, Slit, Stab, Sting, Strike, Swipe, Traumatise, Weaken, Wing, Wrong

140

Wrap   Circumscribe, Clasp, Cover, Embrace,
Enclose, Enfold, Envelop, Enwrap,
Muffle, Protect, Shroud, Surround,
Swathe

Wreathe   Decorate, Encircle, Enfold

Wreck   Debauch, Destroy, Devastate, Mangle,
Plunder, Ravage, Ravish, Ruin, Shatter

Wrench   Force, Grab, Pull, Tug, Twist, Yank

Wrest   Detach, Pull, Ruin, Tug, Twist, Wring

Wring   Twist, Wrest

Wrong   Abuse, Cheat, Discredit, Dishonour,
Harm, Hurt, Injure, Maltreat, Wound

W

Yank   Draw, Pull, Tug, Wrench
Yield   Relinquish, Surrender
Yoke   Bind, Chain, Strap

Zap   Destroy, Hit, Kill

Y-Z

Note

For guidelines on how to use these Emotional Groups to kick-start choosing your actions, refer to page p.xxiv of the Introduction.

The Emotional Groups and their subgroups are:

EMOTIONAL GROUPS

A Loving Words

Accept, Accommodate, Admire, Adore, Adorn, Adulate, Assuage

Baptise, Beatify, Beautify, Betroth, Bless

Calm, Caress, Centre, Civilise, Clasp, Cleanse, Clinch, Coddle, Comfort, Compliment, Compose, Condone, Consecrate, Conserve, Console, Cosset, Court, Cradle, Credit, Cuddle, Cup, Cushion

Defrost, Deify, Delight

Emancipate, Embrace, Enamour, Enchant, Encircle, Encompass, Endear, Enfold, Enfranchise, Enjoin, Enlighten, Enrapture, Enrich, Entertain, Enthral, Entrance, Entwine, Envelop, Enwrap, Evacuate, Extol

Fan, Father, Felicitate, Forgive, Foster

Gladden, Glorify, Grace, Gratify

Hallow, Harmonise, Hold, Honour, Hug

Idolise, Inflame, Infuse, Insure

Jolly

Kindle, Kiss

Level, Liberate, Lick, Lull, Lure

Massage, Melt, Mend, Mollify, Mollycoddle, Mother

Name, Nibble, Nourish, Nurse, Nuzzle

Ornament

Pacify, Pamper, Pardon, Parent, Pat, Paw, Peck, Perfect, Pet, Placate, Please, Pleasure, Praise, Prize, Propitiate, Protect, Purify

Ravish, Rear, Receive, Reconcile, Redeem, Refine, Reform, Regain, Regale, Rehabilitate,

147

Rekindle, Relax, Release, Relieve, Relinquish, Relish, Remedy, Renew, Replenish, Rescue, Respect, Restore, Resuscitate, Retrieve, Revere, Revitalise, Revive, Rock, Romance, Rouse

Safeguard, Salvage, Sanctify, Satiate, Satisfy, Saturate, Save, Savour, School, Secure, Seduce, Select, Serve, Settle, Shepherd, Shield, Shroud, Smoothe, Sober, Soothe, Spellbind, Squeeze, Still, Stroke, Suffuse, Sustain, Swathe

Tease, Temper, Thank, Thaw, Titillate, Titivate, Toast, Touch, Transfix, Transform, Transport, Treasure, Treat

Unburden, Unchain, Unfasten, Unfetter, Unify, Unite, Unravel, Unshackle, Untie

Validate, Value, Venerate, Vindicate, Vitalise

Waken, Warm, Wash, Wean, Wed, Welcome, Win, Woo, Worship

B Encouraging Words

Absolve, Accelerate, Accustom, Acknowledge, Activate, Aggrandise, Amend, Animate, Applaud, Approve, Arouse, Assist, Augment

Befriend, Bestir, Blazon, Bolster, Boost, Brighten

Cajole, Certify, Champion, Coach, Coax, Compel, Compensate, Condition, Congratulate, Conjure, Convert, Correct, Cue, Cultivate

Decorate, Delegate, Designate, Develop, Distinguish, Drill, Drive

Elate, Elect, Electrify, Elevate, Emblazon, Employ, Empower, Enable, Encourage, Endorse, Energise, Engage, Engross, Enkindle, Enlarge, Enlist, Enliven, Excite, Exhilarate

Familiarise, Feed, Fire, Focus, Forward, Fortify, Free, Freshen, Fuel, Further

Greet, Groom, Guide

Habituate, Harden, Hasten, Heal, Heighten, Help

Ignite, Imbue, Impassion, Impel, Implore,
Improve, Include, Incorporate, Induce,
Induct, Infect, Inflate, Influence, Inspire,
Inspirit, Instruct, Intrigue, Invigorate,
Invite, Invoke, Involve

Join

Kindle

Launch, Lead, Lecture, Lift, Light, Lighten

Magnetise, Mobilise, Motivate, Move

Nudge

Organise, Orientate, Overhaul

Permit, Persuade, Polish, Press, Pressure,
Prod, Promote, Prompt, Propel, Pull, Pursue, Push

Quicken

Rally, Reassemble, Reassure, Recommend,
Recondition, Reconstitute, Recruit, Refresh,
Regenerate, Reinvigorate, Rejuvenate, Repair,
Revolutionise, Reward, Rush

Second, Shape, Sharpen, Sophisticate, Spare,
Spark, Spur, Steer, Stiffen, Stimulate, Stir,
Stoke, Strengthen, Stretch, Sweeten, Swell

Tantalise, Teach, Thrill, Thrust, Toughen,
Train, Trigger, Tug, Tutor

Urge, Usher

Warrant

C *Supporting Words*

Abet, Acclaim, Accommodate, Accompany,
Adopt, Advise, Aid, Alert, Allay, Allign,
Anchor, Appoint, Approve, Arm, Assure,
Attend, Authorise, Aver, Award

Back, Balance, Bear, Behold, Bind, Bolster, Brief

Carry, Catch, Cement, Champion, Choose,
Commend, Confirm, Contain, Corroborate,
Counsel, Crown

Defend, Direct, Disburden, Discipline

Embed, Emend, Endorse, Ennoble, Entrust, Equip, Esteem

Fix, Follow, Fortify, Furnish

Generate, Govern, Grasp, Guard, Guide

Hail, Heal, Help, Host, House

Inoculate, Insulate, Inure

Knight

Legitimise, Lift, Lighten, Lodge

Manage, Master, Match

Navigate, Nominate

Obey, Ordain

Pardon, Pay, Pick, Plant, Police, Proclaim

Qualify

Ratify, Rebuild, Receive, Recompense, Reinforce, Remunerate, Retain, Root, Rule

Safeguard, Sponsor, Stabilise Steady, Stoke, Stress

Toast, Trumpet

Uphold, Uplift

Will

A Manipulating Words

Allure, Amaze, Amuse, Appease, Arrest, Attract

Bait, Beg, Beguile, Beseech, Besiege, Bewitch, Bind, Blackmail, Brainwash, Bribe, Browbeat, Buff, Butter

Change, Charm, Churn, Coerce, Corner, Corrupt

Dazzle, Deactivate, Deconstruct

Engineer, Ensnare, Entice, Entrap, Exploit

Fascinate, Flatter, Fondle, Force, Fragment

Hog, Hoodwink, Hook, Humble, Hurry, Hush, Hustle, Hypnotise

Judge, Jumble

Lobby, Lower, Lull

Manipulate, Manoeuvre, Mesmerise, Milk, Monopolise, Mould

Negate

Operate, Outwit, Overcome, Overhaul, Overmaster, Own

Preoccupy, Pressurise, Probe, Programme

Ration, Rush

Sabotage, Seduce, Shake, Solicit, Stump, Subjugate, Suspend

Tempt, Test, Tie, Tighten, Trump

Undermine, Use

Vet, Vilify

B Deceiving Words

Adulterate

Bamboozle, Betray, Blind, Bluff

Cheat, Con, Corrupt

Deceive, Delude, Diddle, Dupe

Entrap

Flatter, Fleece, Foil, Fool

Hoax, Hoodwink, Humour

Kid

Lampoon

Malign, Manoeuvre, Misdirect, Misguide, Mislead, Muddle, Mystify

Pilfer, Pinch, Pluck, Procure, Purloin, Puzzle

Rag

Snare, Steal, Swindle

Throw, Trick, Trip, Trump

Undercut, Undermine

C Disturbing Words

Abandon, Accost, Addle, Affright, Aggravate, Agitate, Alarm, Alert, Annoy, Antagonise,

Badger, Baffle, Bedevil, Benumb, Bewilder, Bother, Bug

Concern, Confine, Confound, Confront, Confuse, Constrain, Contest

Daze, Decline, Deny, Derail, Derange, Deride, Destabilise, Discomfort, Disconcert, Disengage, Dislodge, Displace, Disrupt, Distract, Distress, Disturb, Dominate, Domineer

Elude, Embroil, Encumber, Engulf, Enmesh

Floor, Flummox, Fluster, Freeze, Frighten, Frustrate

Goad, Grab, Grill

Harangue, Haunt, Heckle, Hector, Horrify

Incense, Infect, Infuriate, Interrogate, Interrupt, Irritate

Jolt

Menace, Mortify

Nag, Nauseate

Outrage

Panic, Paw, Peeve, Perplex, Perturb, Pester,
Plague, Poke, Provoke, Puzzle

Query, Question, Quiz

Rattle, Reproach, Reprove, Repulse, Revile,
Ridicule, Rile, Rock, Ruffle

Segregate, Shame, Shock, Sicken, Slight, Snub,
Soil, Spook, Stagger, Stalk, Startle, Stifle,
Stultify, Stump, Stun, Stupefy,
Surprise, Surround, Swamp

Taint, Tarnish, Terrify, Terrorise, Thwart,
Traumatise, Twist

Uncover, Undermine, Undo, Unhinge,
Unhook, Unnerve, Unsettle, Unsteady,
Upset

Vex

Wobble, Wrench, Wrest, Wring

A *Discouraging Words*

Abandon, Admonish, Alienate, Appal, Apprehend, Arraign, Avert, Avoid

Ban, Bar, Belittle, Blight, Block

Cage, Castigate, Censor, Chastise, Chide, Chill, Chop, Chuck, Clutch, Convict, Cool, Cramp, Criticise, Curb

Dampen, Dash, Deactivate, Debilitate, Deflate, Deflect, Deject, Demoralise, Demote, Denigrate, Denounce, Deplete, Depreciate, Depress, Detain, Deter, Dim, Disappoint, Disarm, Discard, Disclaim, Discourage, Disenchant, Disenthrall, Disillusion, Dismay, Dispirit, Disregard, Divert, Dodge, Dull, Dump

Enervate, Enfeeble, Evade, Exclude

Gag

Halt, Hamper, Handicap, Hassle, Henpeck, Hinder, Hound

Ignore, Impeach, Impede, Imperil, Inconvenience, Inhibit, Insult, Intercept, Irk, Irritate, Isolate

Jeopardise, Jibe, Jilt

Leave, Limit

Manacle, Mock, Muffle, Mute, Muzzle

Nettle, Neutralise, Niggle, Nip

Obscure, Obstruct, Offend, Oppose, Ostracise, Overlook

Pan, Parry, Police, Postpone, Prohibit, Prosecute, Punish

Rebuff, Rebuke, Refuse, Reject, Renounce, Repel, Repress, Repudiate, Resist, Restrain, Restrict, Retard, Revoke

Damaging Words

155

Sadden, Saddle, Sap, Scorn, Shirk, Shoulder,
Shove, Shun, Sidestep, Silence, Sop, Sour, Stall,
Stop, Straddle, Suppress

Thwart, Tolerate

B Harming Words

Abduct, Abuse, Accuse, Afflict, Aggrieve,
Assail, Assault, Attack

Bang, Bash, Batter, Battle, Beat, Befoul, Belittle,
Belt, Berate, Besmear, Bind, Birch, Bite,
Blacken, Blame, Blemish, Blight, Block, Boot,
Bowdlerise, Box, Brand, Broach, Browbeat,
Bruise, Brutalise, Bully, Bump, Burden, Burst

Castigate, Castrate, Chain, Chasten, Chastise,
Cheapen, Chide, Chip, Cleave, Clip, Confute,
Crack, Craze, Criticise, Crumple, Cudgel,
Curse, Cuss, Cut

Damage, Dash, Deaden, Debauch, Debilitate,
Deceive, Decry, Defame, Degrade, Demean,
Denigrate, Denounce, Deprave, Deprecate,
Desecrate, Desert, Devalue, Devitalise, Dilute,
Diminish, Disable, Discredit, Disempower,
Dismember, Disgrace, Disown, Dissolve, Drain,
Drown

Eject, Elbow, Embarrass, Embitter, Endanger,
Enfeeble, Enrage, Enslave, Envenom, Expose,
Expropriate

Fatigue, Fetter, Fight, Flail, Fling, Flog, Foul,
Fracture

Gash, Gouge

Harass, Harm, Harry, Hijack, Hit, Humiliate,
Hurt

Immobilise, Impair, Imperil, Impound,
Impoverish, Imprison, Inactivate, Incapacitate,
Incarcerate, Incise, Incriminate, Indict, Infest,
Injure, Intimidate, Invade, Invalidate

Jade, Jeer, Job, Jostle

Kick, Kidnap, Knock

Madden, Maim, Malign, Maltreat, Manacle, Mangle, Manhandle, Mar, Mark, Mimic, Misjudge, Mishandle, Mistreat, Misuse, Molest, Mug

Nab, Nail, Nark, Needle, Neglect, Net, Nick, Notch, Numb

Offend, Oppress, Outlaw, Overload, Overthrow, Overturn, Overwhelm

Paralyse, Patronise, Penetrate, Perforate, Pervert, Pester, Petrify, Pierce, Pillage, Pinch, Pinion, Plunge, Poison, Pollute, Pound, Prick, Prod, Profane, Pummel, Punch, Puncture, Punish

Raid, Ram, Rap, Ravage, Reduce, Repress, Rival, Rob, Ruin

Saddle, Sap, Scar, Scare, Scold, Score, Scratch, Seize, Shackle, Slam, Slander, Slap, Slash, Sling, Slit, Smack, Smash, Smear, Smite, Snare, Snatch, Sock, Soil, Spank, Spike, Splinter, Split, Spoil, Squash, Stab, Stain, Stalk, Starve, Stifle, Strip, Subdue, Submerge, Subsume, Suspend, Swipe

Tackle, Taunt, Thrash, Throttle, Thump, Thwack, Tire, Trample, Trash

Violate, Vitiate

Warn

C Destroying Words

Abolish, Annihilate, Avenge

Banish, Blast, Bludgeon, Break, Bulldoze, Burn, Bury, Bust, Butcher

Conquer, Crucify, Crumble, Crush

Deck, Deflower, Deform, Dehumanise, Desolate, Destroy, Dethrone, Devastate, Devour

Efface, Eliminate, Exterminate, Extinguish, Extirpate

Finish, Flail

Hack, Hawk, Hunt

Immolate, Impale, Incinerate

Kill, Knife

Lacerate, Lash, Lynch

Mash, Massacre, Mince, Murder, Mutilate

Nullify

Obliterate, Oust

Peel, Persecute, Plague, Plunder, Prostrate, Pulverise

Quash, Quell

Ransack, Rape, Ravage, Raze, Ruin, Rule

Sabotage, Sack, Sacrifice, Savage, Scour, Sever, Shatter, Silence, Sink, Skewer, Skin, Slaughter, Smash, Snap, Stab, Stone, Storm, Stuff, Sunder, Suppress, Surrender

Terminate, Topple, Torment, Torture

Vanquish

Wreck